THE
HUNGRY
INHERIT

Whetting Your Appetite for God

THE
HUNGRY
INHERIT

Whetting Your Appetite for God

Zane C. Hodges

MULTNOMAH PRESS
PORTLAND, OREGON 97266

This volume is cordially dedicated to Harold Poole, with the prayer that he might find a rich place in the kingdom of God.

Unless otherwise indicated,
all Scriptures used are the author's paraphrases
of the King James Version of the Bible.

Cover and text illustrations by Don Muth

THE HUNGRY INHERIT
© 1980 by Multnomah Press
Portland, Oregon

Second Edition
Second Printing 1981
Printed in the United States of America

Library of Congress Cataloging in Publication Data

Hodges, Zane Clark.
    The hungry inherit.

        1. Salvation. 2. Christian life - - 1960 -
I. Title.
BT751.2H57 1980   234   80-23676
ISBN 0-930014-50-2

Contents

Foreword

Seldom in one book are combined the really important features that are found in this one, and seldom is truth presented so attractively and faithfully.

The burden of this work is to distinguish clearly salvation and discipleship. No distinction is more vital to theology, more basic to a correct understanding of the New Testament, or more relevant to every believer's life and witness. The distinction is introduced through two of our Lord's earliest conversations; and it is reinforced by references to the teachings of James, Paul, and John, which are portrayed on the background of other incidents in the life of Christ. When one finishes this book, there can be no mistaking the fact that the free gift of the water of life and the call to discipleship are clearly distinguished in the New Testament.

No dry theology is this, for Professor Hodges uses a story-telling method as he unfolds the truth of various passages. Only the need to take time to digest the solid meat that is in each chapter will make the reader put this book down before finishing it. Mr. Hodges is completely qualified in the technical aspects of this work, and his colleagues and students will find in the book the same fascinating style he displays in his oral ministry.

Because we live in a day where the water of life is sometimes clouded with human works, even by evangelicals, the message of this book needs to be heralded far and wide. As one who is known to share the convictions expressed in this work,

I am very grateful to God for its publication. May it be widely read and used of the Lord to clarify and exalt His matchless grace.

CHARLES C. RYRIE

Dallas Theological Seminary

Introduction

Come with us to Palestine, a tiny land only a trifle larger than the state of Vermont, and join us at the site of an ancient well near the little village of Sychar. An important conversation is about to take place there, which has drastically affected the lives of untold thousands down through the ages.

In fact, Palestine is the world's greatest stage. For on that stage there has been enacted history's most significant drama. And though it happened long ago, its relevance to men in these days is as great—and greater—than the headlines in tomorrow morning's papers. There is not a man alive who can escape the crucial questions with which that drama—right here and now—confronts him.

We don't want to just tell you about the drama. We want you to be a part of it. We want you to meet its actors, and to hear their voices. Above all, we want you to think their thoughts and feel their feelings. Only in this way, perhaps, can the momentous issues which are involved be clothed with flesh and blood. For the people in this story are made of flesh and blood. They lived and breathed, and talked and ate, and felt and believed. They are real people in a real world facing real questions which we must face today as well.

Of course, you will not find *all* the scenes of this drama comprehended within the pages of this book. For that, you must consult the Bible itself. But if you look closely you will find here two great themes which run like interwoven threads throughout the entirety of the drama and give color and character even to the parts of it which are not herein described. It would be impossible to exaggerate the importance of these kindred themes. They are central to man's search for the meaning of his life.

You will need a little imagination as you read this book. For the pictures painted here are not only those of an ancient land and culture, but more especially of the hearts and minds of men who wrestled with staggering realities. No one can paint such pictures perfectly, and we have only done the best we could. Yet if there are details of the portrait which another might draw with somewhat different strokes, the twin truths which the portrait is designed to set off are sure and certain. And it is to these that we are basically calling the reader's attention.

What are these truths? To answer that here would be to get ahead of our story. We must take one step at a time. So for now, it is on to Sychar.

1

Discovering the Gift of God

John 4:1-29

> *If thou knewest the gift of God, and who it is that saith to thee, Give me to drink; thou wouldest have asked of him, and he would have given thee living water* (Jn 4:10).

The declining Palestinian sun beat down warmly on a tired and dusty traveler who wearily sat on the large stone which covered the shaft of a Middle Eastern well. In the background loomed the slope of Mount Gerizim, rich with the ancient traditions of the Samaritan people, in whose territory the traveler now found Himself. In the foreground rose the even higher peak of Mount Ebal, at the foot of which was nestled the tiny Samaritan village of Sychar. The well that the traveler sat upon stood just beyond the mouth of the narrow valley which ran between the mountain ridges of Gerizim and Ebal, a valley which opened out to His right into a vast plain covered with rapidly ripening grain fields.

Though exhausted by the long journey from Judea in the south, the alert eyes of the traveler scanned the landscape to His north as though searching for someone or something for which He waited. Presently His attentive gaze was rewarded by the lone figure of a woman, waterjar mounted securely on her head, making her way in the direction of the well. His eyes followed her approaching steps, and the flicker of a look of compassion passed briefly over His sweat-streaked countenance.

At length she had arrived before Him. To her surprise, He addressed her.

"Give me a drink," Jesus said.

"How does it happen," the woman replied, "that You—a Jew—are asking for a drink from me—a Samaritan woman?"

Her question was no idle one, for she knew well the deep scorn with which the women of Samaria were regarded by the ordinary Jewish man. And the features of the man before her, His Galilean brogue, marked Him plainly as a Jew. Why then this request? A scrupulous man of His race would not think of using the same drinking vessel as a woman of hers.

But the social question she had raised was of no moment on this occasion. That was an external consideration only, and it was with matters deeper and far more penetrating than this that the man before her was concerned. He did not even pause to answer her question.

"If only," He continued, "you had known the gift of God and who it was that said to you, 'Give Me a drink,' *you* would have asked a drink of *Him,* and He would have given you living water."

The woman was not so sure she agreed with that. What could induce her to ask *Him* for a drink? After all, she had her own waterpot and came daily to this well. She had not needed assistance before and felt she did not need it now. Furthermore it seemed quite irrelevant at the moment to talk about some gift from God. Whatever that might be, it had nothing to do with the problem of filling her waterpot.

Of course, the woman did not understand Him. In the language they were using, the words "living water" signified *flowing* water such as that which supplied the deep well on which Jesus was sitting.

"Sir," she responded quizzically, "You don't have a bucket and the well is deep. Where then do You get this flowing water? Surely You aren't greater than our father Jacob who gave us this well and drank of it himself with his family and cattle, are You?"

There was a note of sarcasm in her voice now. To dig a well to which supplies of water would be both copious and long-lasting in the arid East was no small accomplishment indeed. Jacob's well met both these conditions, for its resources had been adequate not only for his sizable household and for his numerous flocks and herds, but more than this, its waters had continued to flow through the centuries right down to this very day. And that was why the woman was here. "He gave *us* this well," she said. "Are You great enough to do better?"

He *was* great enough. But this was not the moment to tell her so. True, a basic datum which He must shortly impart to her involved His divine identity, and the revelation of that identity would make it as pointless to compare Jacob with Him as it is pointless to compare a candle with the sun. But first, she must know the gift of God. This well was Jacob's gift. The gift of God, however, was of an entirely different order; and this fact must be stated at once.

"Anyone who drinks of this water will get thirsty again," replied the Saviour, ignoring Jacob entirely. "But whoever takes a drink of the water that I will give him, will never thirst! In fact, the water that I will give him will become inside of him a spring of water gushing up into eternal life!"

The offer was staggering! No water from this, or any other earthly well, could produce such a result. In fact, every drink —of whatever kind—that the world offered to thirsty man could have only the most fleeting and transient effect. And if that was true of all the literal waters used to temporarily quench man's physical thirst, it was much more poignantly true of the worldly fountains at which they sought to quench their thirst of heart.

Love, success, wealth, fame—these were but a few of the countless springs at which men had stooped to drink, only to

rise from them to find that they offered no lasting inward satisfaction, no enduring personal fulfillment. "Whoever drinks of
this water shall thirst again," was a statement as broad as the
innumerable means by which men had sought their ultimate
contentment.

But His water was different! It could accomplish a miracle!
The one who drank it was secure from thirst, not merely for
time but for eternity as well. "Whoever drinks of this water
will *never* thirst!" The need that His water was designed to
meet and for which men were to appropriate it, was a need
that could never reoccur. Thus, in its infinitely satisfying
qualities, it exceeded the value of any earthly drink as much as
the value of an ingot of pure gold exceeds the value of a speck
of sand.

But how could it do this? The answer was both simple and
mysterious. This water, when appropriated, *became* something
within the one who appropriated it. "The water that I will give
him *shall become in him* a spring of water gushing up to eternal
life." So vital, so transforming was such a drink, that in the
innermost being of the man who drank it, there was created
an inexhaustible fountain of life. The waters of that hidden
inner spring could not run dry; they could not be stanched;
they virtually leaped up to produce the surpassing experience
of eternal life. There could be no question, then, of needing
more than a single drink. Deep though Jacob's well was, and
though its waters had flowed continuously for many centuries,
the drinker of that water must return again and again. For
Jacob's spring was in the earth, external to the one who sought
it. But the Saviour's spring was within the heart, continuously
meeting the need of one who drank but a single time.

"Are You greater than our father Jacob who gave us this
well?"

He *had* to be. Man might dig wells in the earth. Only God
could dig one in the human heart!

But the woman once more missed the point. "Sir," she

replied, "give me this water so that I won't get thirsty nor be coming back here to draw!"

It was as much a challenge as a request. It would be easy enough to test this fantastic offer. Let Him give her a drink! It wouldn't be long before she discovered whether His water had the staying powers He claimed for it. And after all, it *would* be nice to eliminate this well from her daily itinerary! Life would at least be a trifle more simple!

But Jesus had not offered her that. The elimination of physical and temporal needs was not the purpose of His coming nor the goal of this interview. He had never said she would not have to come back here to draw water. His offer dealt with her spiritual and eternal need. And until she could think with Him in those terms, she could not make her request aright. Clearly, the conversation needed a new focus.

"Go call your husband and come back," said Jesus.

An embarrassed moment of silence ensued. "I don't have a husband," she blurted out.

"You're quite right you don't have a husband," continued Jesus calmly. "The fact is you have had five of them, but the man you're living with now is not your husband. Here at least you said something true."

This was quite unexpected. Also quite unwelcome. How did He know all this? She'd never seen Him before in her life. She was both curious and uncomfortable. How could she pursue the conversation in a manner less painful to her sensibilities? Then a thought struck her.

"I can tell, Sir, that You're a prophet. Our fathers worshiped in this mountain." She nodded toward Gerizim behind Him. "But you people say that Jerusalem is the place where men ought to worship."

It was skillfully done. If He were nothing more than an ordinary Jew, He would only give her the ordinary Jewish answer, perhaps even a religious tirade, for she knew how explosive the subject was. Yet she could no longer resist the feeling that His answer to this question might be just as striking as His comment on her life. This was no ordinary man. Might He not have an unlooked-for wisdom on the very point she had raised?

Her expectation was not disappointed. She had raised the subject of worship, and the Saviour's reply was as pregnant a statement on this theme as had ever escaped the lips of man. Indeed, once He had uttered it, it would be impossible thereafter for any man intelligently to ponder this theme without returning to consider those priceless words. As an utterance on worship they were timeless and absolutely definitive.

"Woman," said Jesus, "believe Me! The hour is coming when neither in this mountain," He too nodded toward Gerizim, "nor yet at Jerusalem will you people worship the Father. You people are worshiping what you don't know. We know what we worship. After all, salvation is of the Jews."

Here's a new approach! the woman could not help thinking. A Jew who was willing to dismiss Jerusalem along with Gerizim! That was novel! Yet He insisted on the Jewish origin of salvation, and that was *not* novel. Still, she was intrigued.

Jesus was continuing. "But an hour is coming, yes it is now here, when the real worshipers will worship the Father in spirit and in truth. In fact, the Father actually seeks such people as His worshipers."

So that's it, she thought. This man was telling her that God was not satisfied with the worship either of Gerizim *or* Jerusalem. He looked for *real* worshipers, not the kind whose pious prayers and religious platitudes hypocritically cloaked the pride and covetousness of their hearts. There was all too much of that at Gerizim, she knew, and there must be a great deal more at Jerusalem as well. At least, she was quite ready to believe there was.

"God is spirit," the Saviour's answer went on, "and those who worship Him must worship in spirit and in truth."

He paused, and so did she. It seemed that a new vista of

truth had been opened up before her eyes, though just now she could but dimly see some of its terrain. Yet His words had the ring of self-evident truth. God, she knew, was indeed a spiritual being. How then could a material mountain—like Gerizim—or a lavishly adorned structure—like the temple at Jerusalem—have any real or enduring importance to such a being? Was it not the heart of man that God searched? Was it not truth that He sought in man's inward parts? Was it not with the spirit of man, which He Himself had made, that the Creator sought communion? And was it not plain, then, that if He were to be worshiped at all, He *must* be worshiped "in spirit and in truth"?

Yes, it was plain. But so was something else. The prophet-like person before her, who knew so well—*too* well—the unhappy succession of liaisons she had formed with five men, only to be living now in adultery with a sixth, spoke of worship as though it pertained to her and her fellow Samaritans.

"The hour is coming when neither in this mountain nor yet at Jerusalem will *you people* worship the Father," He had said. Indeed, the hour was here already, He had affirmed. Might it not be then, after all, that He Himself was an emissary of the Father-God about whom He spoke, whose mission it was to seek worshipers for this God? And might it not be as well (The thought staggered her!) that *she* was one of those whom He thus sought?

But how could she ever approach the infinite and eternal Spirit who desired her worship? Her own spirit, it seemed, was irrevocably soiled by the baseness of her life, hopelessly dried up by the emptiness of an existence strewn with the wreckage of marriage upon marriage. She could find nothing in her heart or life that might serve as a viable point of contact with a living God.

Then she remembered it. The *water!* "Flowing" water, she had thought at first, but the word He had used meant "living" as well. *Living* water! Water gushing up to eternal life. Life producing life throughout all ages; one drink, therefore, satisfying her need for such life once and for all; bringing her then into living contact with God; washing away the barrenness of her heart, granting her the capacity to *worship*. The thoughts rushed in upon her all at once. She could not quite sort them out. But now she *had* to ask Him a question.

"Salvation is of the Jews," He had said. And *He* was a Jew. He had also offered her life—eternal life—were she but to ask for it. Could He be—? Was He—?

"I know," replied the woman, "that Messiah, the one called Christ, is coming." She hesitated to put the question directly, but it *was* a question. "When He comes, He will tell us all things." *And,* she thought, *could He tell us more than this man about worship?*

She was ready for the answer, and the Saviour spoke it with climactic succinctness. "I," He said, "the one who is speaking to you, am He!"

Not one further word was spoken. Like the sun bursting forth from behind the clouds, the light of truth had flooded her soul. She turned from Him, the waterjar she had come to fill standing empty upon the ground, but the heart she had not come to fill now overflowing with living water. She must tell the people of her city who was here, before He passed from them. She must go back. And so she quickly retreated along the path by which she had come, while the Son of God, still seated upon the well, watched her go.

"If thou knewest the gift of God, and who it is that saith to thee, Give me to drink; thou wouldest have asked of him, and he would have given thee living water." Ignorant she had come, enlightened she had left. Empty she had arrived, full she had departed. The gift of God? She knew it now—eternal life inexhaustibly welling up within the heart! "Who it is that saith to thee, 'Give me to drink' "? She knew *Him* now—the Christ, the Saviour of the world!

She knew these two things. They were all she needed to

know, deftly led to them by the skill of the Saviour. Then a transaction had occurred. Without a word, without a prayer, her heart had asked and He had given. *"Thou wouldest have asked of him, and he would have given thee living water."*

2

True Spiritual Food

John 4:27-39

*In the mean while his disciples prayed him, saying, Master,
eat. But he said unto them, I have meat to eat that ye know
not of* (Jn 4:31-32).

The waterjar stood there perfectly empty and completely
forgotten. The woman who had carried it to this spot was
now gone, excitedly announcing her startling discovery to the
incredulous villagers of Sychar. Often before, on innumerable
days just like this one, she had drawn out the water of Jacob's
well, and by now its taste and appearance were so familiar to
her that she no longer really noticed them. But on *this* day,
she had found at that well—though not *in* it—a new kind of
water, totally unfamiliar to her before.

The same well was now surrounded by Jesus' disciples. The
foodstuffs which they had gone off into Sychar to purchase were
rapidly emerging from the bulging traveler's sacks of leather
which they wore at their left hip, fastened by a strap over the
right shoulder. They were eager to eat. Only momentarily had
they been deflected from this purpose. For, a few moments
before, they had managed to arrive just as their Master was
concluding His interview with the woman of Sychar, and they
had had difficulty concealing their shock.

They knew quite well that no respectable Jewish rabbi allowed himself to engage in public conversation with a woman,

and they had been astounded by the obvious impropriety of the situation they had found. Yet their respect for their teacher was too deep to permit them to voice any word of censure. They had been sorely tempted to ask some question like, "Why are You talking to her?" or "What are You after?" but that would have sounded critical, and so they had kept silent. Nevertheless, their puzzlement had been real.

Just now, however, they could almost forget that. The long day's journey had left them all hungry, and the provisions over which they had haggled with the Samaritan merchants looked at this moment as if they were worth every penny of their exorbitant price.

It was not for themselves alone they had bought, however, but for their teacher as well. By now they knew His tastes, and these they had kept in mind while they negotiated in Sychar's marketplace. Moreover, deference to Him as their rabbi forbade them to eat their own food before He should begin to partake of His. It was, therefore, with a mixture of true consideration and of self-concern that they now offered Him some of their choicest purchases.

"Master, eat!" they said. They were not prepared for the reply.

Only a short time before, a woman had discovered on this very spot the *water* that she knew not of. Now it was the disciples' turn to make a different discovery. What the woman had learned at the well that day, the disciples had learned a number of months before. The one to whom they now offered physical nourishment was already known to them as He had not been known to the woman. He was the Christ, the Son of the living God, and from the moment they had recognized this fact they had possessed the same gift of God as that which had just been bestowed on the sinful citizeness of Sychar. Therefore, they were no strangers to life eternal. Deep within their inner selves there had been opened up some time ago the same limitless fountain of life that had sprung into being in that other heart right where they now stood. And no more could that experience be repeated for them than it could be repeated for the woman. But of another matter they remained quite ignorant.

Jesus answered them, "I have food to eat that you don't know about!"

How could that be? He carried no provisions of His own. Had He had some other encounter while they were gone, with someone besides the woman? So far as they had observed, she had given Him nothing. "Someone hasn't brought Him something to eat, has he?" they inquired dubiously of each other. Obviously, on one point there could be no debate. Whatever food it was their Master spoke about, it was food they *knew not of!* As surely as the woman had been ignorant of His water, *they* were ignorant of His food.

Their teacher had paused to allow them to puzzle over His statement. When He saw that they had exhausted the limited explanations they could conceive, He was ready to instruct them further.

"My food," said Jesus, "is to do the will of the One who sent Me, and to finish His work."

Here indeed was a new theme altogether. Doing the will of God! Finishing His work! Not a word of these matters had been spoken to the woman, though how well it would seem they might have been. Clearly the life she had lived up until she met Jesus, had done shameful and inexcusable violence to the will of God for her. Yet, Jesus had said nothing about the repair of her life which, plainly, was so urgently needed.

It was not that He did not *care*—no one cared more than He. But He knew He would see her again. There would be time for further instruction, just as now He was instructing His disciples. But in those moments when she stood before Him at the well, He had said nothing of her obligations to God's will for a very simple reason: He was there to offer her a *gift.* "If thou knewest the gift of God" had been His theme. And she could not have comprehended the dazzling splendor of that gift, its sublime and total freeness, had He encumbered His offer with a call to reform her life.

Indeed, in that interview before the well, it was not the moment for Jesus to be concerned that *she* should do the will of God. Rather it was the moment to be concerned that He should do the will of God. And if the Father longed for worshipers, who would worship Him in spirit and in truth, to do the Father's will the Son must seek them. It was God's will, therefore, that the parched and arid ground of a guilty woman's heart should taste that day the refreshing streams of life eternal. The universe has no greater gift for man than this, nor any greater impulse to thankful worship than that which reception of this gift imparts. And so, at Jacob's well, Jesus did the will of God.

But what did the disciples know of this? Nothing really. That the need of their own souls had been satisfied was true enough. But to satisfy God? To find worshipers for Him? To eat and enjoy that task, as one eats and enjoys food? *That* was food that they knew not of!

Strangely enough, the woman herself seemed almost intuitively to have begun to learn the lesson on which the disciples required such specific instruction. No sooner had she abandoned her unfilled waterjar and rushed back into the village from which she had come, than she began to proclaim her experience to others.

"Come," she said to the men of Sychar, "see a man who told me all the things I ever did. Is this perhaps the Christ?"

"Is this perhaps the Christ?" Her caution was instinctively judicious. Had she frontally asserted the truth about which she had become convinced, she might have repelled them. Her notorious life was common knowledge in that city. So they had not mistaken her cautious approach for a lack of conviction. Oblique though it had been, it was effective. The curiosity of the village was aroused. And while the Lord Jesus was preparing His disciples to partake of His food, a company of the men of Sychar were making their way back to the well to partake of His water! The Son of God was still sitting on the stone which covered the shaft of Jacob's well. Before Him stretched a vast expanse of waving grain, its rapidly ripening ears gently moved by an evening breeze. But the keen eyes of the Saviour saw other movement as well. The company from Sychar had begun to leave the village, making its way rapidly toward the well. Visually, the harvest of men and the harvest of God, for a few moments at least, had merged.

Jesus continued speaking to His disciples. "Isn't it your habit to say, 'There are still four months before harvest comes'? Nevertheless I say to you, lift up your eyes and look at the fields, because they are white for harvesting already."

In the fertile plain of Samaria on which the eyes of Jesus rested, the four months between seedtime and harvest had already elapsed. The patience with which the Palestinian farmer resigned himself to the cycle of nature, expressed so aptly at sowing time by the observation that four months must pass before the fruit, was now once again about to be rewarded. The fields were white and ready to harvest.

Yet, in the harvest field of God, no such lapse of time was needed. The good seed of the Saviour's word had already brought forth fruit in the heart of a sinful woman. And now, in turn, the seed of her words to the villagers of Sychar was about to bear even more abundant fruit. The approaching company of men, after only the briefest cultivation, was ready to be reaped into God's barn.

But harvesting is not done without work. Effort must be expended by the reaper to gather in the crop. If the divine harvest field was ripe, the divine will was that it should be reaped. And reaped completely! Not merely one needy woman must be brought into God's barn, but many more from the village where she lived. "My food," Jesus had said, "is to do the will of Him that sent Me, and *to finish His work."*

The soul of the Saviour had already tasted the spiritual nourishment which came as He imparted the gift of life to one sinner. That was the will of God for Him. But the work must be completed, the field of Sychar thoroughly harvested. And Jesus is now prepared to invite the disciples to share that task with Him, and thus to partake of the food which, until now, they knew not of!

"Furthermore," Jesus continued, "the one who reaps receives wages, and he gathers in fruit to life eternal, so that both the sower and the reaper may rejoice together."

So that was it! A glimmer of light now began to filter its way through into the benighted recesses of the disciples' minds. Fruit gathered in to eternal life! Clearly their teacher was not thinking of an ordinary harvest, though instinctively they had glanced at the ripening grain fields when He first mentioned them. But eternal life was a spiritual reality, not a natural one. It was, they knew, a surpassing experience enjoyed not merely in time but throughout all eternity as well. And the imagery Jesus used suggested to them a new figure for that life. Eternal life, it seemed, was like a vast and spacious barn into which men, like harvested grain, could be gathered for their own eternal preservation. And for this task God wanted reapers. Might He, therefore, want them?

He did! "In this respect," said Jesus, "there is truth in the saying that one is a sower while another is a reaper. I have sent you to reap what you have not labored on. Others have labored, and you have entered into their labors."

Yes, they knew it was so. In the natural world a reaper was not usually the one who had sowed the seed. Indeed, while one man alone might sow an entire field, the handfuls of seed from his seed sack being hurled over the terrain, one man alone could scarcely reap that field when once the crop was ripe. The sower, therefore, looked for help at harvest time, and thus the joys and reward of the harvest were distributed to a wider circle than those who had planted the field.

And now Jesus had said plainly that they had a commission from Him to reap what others alone had sowed. Not that the sowers themselves would cease to be active. But rather the disciples would then participate in the continuing labor.

By now, the crowd from Sychar was clearly visible even to the disciples. The woman they had seen earlier was leading them. Clearly, the conversation Jesus had held with her was responsible for their approach. What had been obscure to them before—even shocking—was now becoming plain. Of course! They should have guessed! Jesus had obviously been talking to this woman about eternal life, just as they had seen Him talk to so many others on the same sublime theme. Indeed, there was nothing He talked about so frequently as that, and they should have known how deeply He felt that such conversation was His way of doing the will of the One who sent Him. But evidently the woman had been talking as well, or these Samaritan men would not be coming to this well. Drawing water was a woman's job and, clearly, they had not come to do that.

The disciples knew what would happen. They would have to forget about supper! They must get ready to talk to these villagers just as Jesus had done with this woman. So they must try to forget how hungry they were!

And then it was all so perfectly clear! "I have food to eat that you don't know about. My food is to do the will of the One who sent Me, and to finish His work." He could easily forget His earthly food, if only He could partake of this spiritual food. If only He could be in God's harvest field reaping souls into eternal life, He could forget anything. And so could they, if they chose to. He had sowed, the woman had sowed, and now it was the disciples' opportunity to enter into those labors. Thus they, too, could do the will of God, and do it till God's work was finished.

"Furthermore, the one who reaps receives wages," Jesus had said. Their effort would be well repaid. The kingdom of God toward which they looked would be a richer place for them if just now they could make some small sacrifice for the will of God. And what after all did their miserable supper count for, when weighed against the honors and glories of that kingdom? Already, they were beginning to sense the exhilaration of the task to which they had been called.

No wonder He could forget to eat. This was better than food! No, that was wrong. This was a better *food!* He had had food to eat that they knew not of. But the crowd from Sychar had just arrived. The inevitable conversation was now beginning. And so also was their opportunity to taste that food!

3

We Are God's Workmanship

John 4:40; Ephesians 2:8-10

> *For by grace are ye saved through faith; and that not of yourselves: it is the gift of God: not of works, lest any man should boast. For we are his workmanship, created in Christ Jesus unto good works, which God hath before ordained that we should walk in them* (Eph 2:8-10).

The sun had now disappeared beneath the horizon, and the shadows of the approaching darkness spread rapidly over the Samaritan landscape. The conversation at the well had had a predictable outcome. The villagers of Sychar had been deeply impressed with this Jewish traveler and had entreated Him to lodge that night in their city. And so Jesus and His disciples were now making their way toward the town in the company of their new-found hosts.

Jacob's well was being left behind, deserted for the first time in hours. The stone which covered its shaft remained unmoved. What a pity that that stone could not speak! What words had been uttered over it that day! Indeed, the words that had been spoken there that day had been of such magnitude and significance that, for those who comprehend them, they are a key which unlocks the Bible.

But only the stone had heard *all* those words! When Jesus had spoken of living water, only the woman had been present. And when He had spoken of unknown food, only the disciples had been present. The water was what the woman needed, and the food was what the disciples needed, and the Saviour carefully segregated His audiences. How important!

Nothing happened by chance in the life of the Son of God. All of the circumstances in which He moved were as perfect as He was Himself. The woman was a sinner, never having experienced that salvation which was "of the Jews." *She* needed the water of life. The disciples had already come to know the Saviour and the salvation He gave. *They* needed the food of obedience to God's will.

The two must never be confused. Water is water, and food is food. And an unsaved sinner is an unsaved sinner, but a disciple is a disciple. Thus, the thirst of a disciple has already been quenched forever. He needs food! Doing the will of God. Finishing His work.

Here, then, is found the very quintessence of the Christian gospel, and the very quintessence of Christian experience. Here, too, are found the differing audiences for which they are each designed. The Christian gospel is the offer of the gift of life directed toward the guilty sinner. Christian experience is the offer of the will of God directed toward the loyal disciple. The former is water, the latter is food. The former guarantees eternal life without end, throughout all ages, to any who will take it. The latter promises reward and superlative joy, like the joy of a great harvest, to all who are willing to expend their labor. The former is a gift. The latter involves work.

Years after the events at Jacob's well, a short, slightly balding man slowly paced the floor of his private quarters. A Roman sentry dozed intermittently in one corner of the room, while a professional scribe sat alertly at his desk, a large papyrus sheet spread open before him and a reed pen poised in his hand.

The short man pacing the floor frowned slightly, his large eyebrows seeming to merge above his sharp, rather prominent nose, as he struggled for words. *How shall I phrase the next utterance? It has to be just right.*

He must make clear to the Christians who would read this letter the exact relationship between the wondrous kindness God had showed in saving them and their unrivaled privilege in serving Him. Not that he had never made it clear before! For two years he had preached and taught in Ephesus, that bustling metropolis of Asia Minor, and those in that place to whom he now wrote had heard him state such truths many times (Ac 19:10; 20:20-21, 27). Yet he knew from long experience in the harvest fields of God that those who were reaped into the divine barn often became confused on these very points. Moreover, there were always the sinister agents of Satan, posing as ministers of the gospel, who cultivated and encouraged such confusion. The facts, therefore, could never be stated too often or too well.

Now the words were beginning to come. He began again to dictate and the scribe began again to write.

"For," said Paul, "by grace you have been saved through faith."

Grace? It was one of his favorite words. Kindness, goodness, mercy, generosity—it signified all these things to him. What a rebel he had been before he knew what that word was all about! Stubbornly rejecting the claim that Jesus of Nazareth was God's Son. Viciously hounding and persecuting all who had trusted in Jesus as the giver of life, the Saviour. Some he had seen imprisoned, others he had seen killed. He had believed, of course, that salvation was of the Jews, but not (certainly not!) of the man called Jesus. Then he had met Him in one blazing, brilliant moment on a highway leading into Damascus. And out of the splendor of a light which exceeded the brightness of the noonday sun, he had heard the answer to his question, "Who are You, Lord?"

The answer had crushed him, but it had revolutionized his life. "I am Jesus, whom you are persecuting!" (Ac 26:9-20).

And now he was a Christian missionary! And an apostle, as well! Was any man ever less deserving of such privileges?

He could not think so. But that was what *grace* meant to him. The superlative goodness of God to the utterly undeserving. And every one of the readers of this letter must be reminded that they too were the beneficiaries of grace. The salvation which they had and the eternal life which they had received had become theirs simply by believing. "By grace you have been saved through faith."

"By grace you have been saved through faith; and that not of yourselves," Paul continued, "it is the gift of God."

The gift of God! How perfect the expression was. How fully in the Spirit of the One Paul had met outside Damascus. For after all, it was not Paul who had first used such a phrase but the Saviour Himself. "If thou knewest the *gift of God,*" Jesus had said to the woman. And unworthy though her life had been, she, like the Ephesians to whom Paul now wrote, had taken God's gift by faith. They had all been saved alike. Indeed, there was no other way to be saved.

"Not of works," Paul went on, "so that no one may boast."

Boast? How was that possible for one who received this gift? Could the woman of Sychar boast that God had singled her out, the first in all her village to possess eternal life, when in the very next breath she must say, "He told me all that I ever did"? Now, if she had promised to *work* for it or if she had guaranteed to *make up* for her sordid, wasted life with *good works,* then, she *might* have boasted. But how could she boast about things as they actually were? She hadn't worked for it, and she couldn't pay for it. It was the *gift* of God! *Not* of works! And why? Just so that the glory might all be God's and no one might usurp that glory.

The woman could not boast. Paul, the one-time persecutor, could not boast. The Ephesian Christians could not boast. No man in all the ages of an endless future will ever be able to boast, for salvation cannot be earned. It is never deserved. It is always the gift of God.

That was the water. What about the food? Paul continued to dictate.

"For we are His workmanship, created in Christ Jesus for good works, which God has prepared ahead of time so that we may walk in them."

Often Paul had seen a potter sitting before the wheel on which he painstakingly shaped vessels of every size and description, carefully molding some object he held firmly but lovingly in his hands. Then he had watched the artisan, when the work on the wheel was done, take a shell or a shard or an instrument of bone, with which he might smooth and burnish or decorate its surface.

The final product of his work—a pitcher or jar or cup or platter—was always an object of pride to a conscientious craftsman, the product of his skill and genius. That vessel, whatever its intended use, was his *workmanship. And so,* thought Paul, *is every person who has been saved by grace.* "For we are *His* workmanship, created in Christ Jesus."

We were most surely not our own workmanship, Paul was thinking. *Our* works had nothing to do with our salvation. Rather we were, by means of the gift of God, the product of the master Potter. Sinners He had found us, a miserable, misshapen mass of earthly clay, and when the transforming touch of His grace had been applied to us, we had a new life in Christ Jesus. We were, in short, a new creation, product of the skill and craft of the eternal Artisan.

But every vessel wrought by an earthly potter has a purpose and function for which it is designed. And so it is with every vessel wrought by the heavenly Potter. "We are His workmanship, created in Christ Jesus *for good works."* Good works, then, were *our* function, the purpose for which He made us. They have nothing to do with the bestowal of God's gift, but they have everything to do with the life which should follow. The water is always *given.* The food is always *worked for.*

So God has created us, Paul was saying, for good works.

But, he adds, He has also created good works for us! "We are His workmanship, created in Christ Jesus for good works, which God *has prepared ahead of time* so that we may walk in them." Nothing is left to chance. The person is designed for the work, and the work is designed for the person. When the water of life has been tasted, divine food will be ready at hand.

"Lift up your eyes and look at the fields," Jesus had said to His disciples, "because they are white for harvesting already!" There it was—God's work for them—right before their eyes, if only they were willing to see it. There it was—God's will for them—ready at hand, if only they were willing to do it!

Life eternal the disciples possessed already. They, too, were God's workmanship. Now the vessel must be employed in the task it was formed for, and in the task that was formed for it. Thus the disciples entered God's harvest field, joining their Master in order to do the will of God and to finish His work. And that was a disciple's special privilege, as it was also his special joy, to be guided by his teacher into the realization of every splendid goal which God has prepared for him to achieve.

The company that left Jacob's well had now entered the village of Sychar. Darkness had fallen, but the conversation continued long into the night. The disciples were weary when at last they were able to throw themselves down on pallets in the home where they were lodged. Tomorrow was likely to be just as busy, for the thirst of that village for the water of life had not yet been quenched. Still more souls were ready to be harvested into God's barn. The morning would come all too quickly.

It was work, to be sure. But ultimately those men would become superbly skilled in doing it. And why not? Was it not one of the very tasks they had been saved to perform? And whether it was this good work or any of the countless other good works their Saviour had designed, the disciples' responsibility was simply "to walk in them."

4

The Life-giving Word

John 4:39-54

And many more believed because of his own word; and said unto the woman, Now we believe, not because of thy saying: for we have heard him ourselves, and know that this is indeed the Christ, the Saviour of the world (Jn 4: 41-42).

The disciples spent two days "walking" with their Master in the good work being done in Sychar. That was how long it took to complete God's harvest in that Samaritan village. The interest of the villagers had been intense—the disciples had not seen anything like it among the Jews—and they seemed literally to hang on every statement Jesus uttered. There were no miracles performed in Sychar, and no one asked for any. All that the Samaritans needed to convince them was His word.

That was, after all, what had convinced the woman at Jacob's well. "Come, see a man who told me all the things I ever did," she had exclaimed, upon rushing back to her village. She had been amazed that this perfect stranger had unrolled before her the entire scroll of her unhappy life. "You're quite right you don't have a husband," Jesus had told her. "The fact is you have had five of them, but the man you're now living with is not your husband." That was her whole life in a nutshell! For nothing else had really mattered to this woman but her vain pursuit of happiness in wedlock, just as nothing else had so thoroughly made her what she was. She did not need a supporting miracle. His word to her was miracle enough. And when He had added those unforgettable pronouncements on the theme of worship, she had been prepared to believe that He was exactly who He claimed to be—God's Christ.

Many of the villagers of Sychar had been equally impressed with His word to her. And when she had explained how "He told me all that I ever did," many of them had believed in Him, agreeing that this must be the Christ. But some preferred to defer their decision until they had heard Him firsthand. And during those two days in Sychar they had had ample opportunity to do just that. Like the woman out at the well, they plied Him with questions and were continually amazed by the wisdom and insight in His answers. Often, it seemed, He did more than answer the questions they had asked. He seemed to be answering the questions they had *not* asked—but wanted to—as though He was reading their hearts. The impact was irresistible. Many more from that village believed in Him.

Then they did an unkind thing. The woman who had aroused their interest in the first place had completely forfeited the respect of her fellow townspeople by the wanton life she had lived. They hated to let her think that, despite her base character, she had led them to the greatest discovery of their lives. Indeed, she might prove intolerable if they permitted her to build up her self-esteem on this point. Better to quash her pride before it had a chance to appear. So now they undertook to do just that.

Those who had previously believed when she had told them Jesus' words to her, and those who had just now believed after having personal audience with Him, were united in their attitude toward the woman. "Now we believe," they assured her, "not because of *your* chatter, but because we have heard Him for ourselves and we know that this really is the Christ, the Saviour of the world!"

The words stung, but it was all right. Her own heart was too full of the joy of the water of life for her to brood over this rejection. And after all, it was not really *her* word that had convinced any of them, but *Jesus'* word to her. She had simply reported it. Whether, therefore, they heard His words through her, or heard them from His own lips personally, it was *His* word that had produced new life in them.

Already, after only two days in His presence, it was evident to her, as it was to every believer in that city, that the word of Jesus was a life-giving word. It could not be otherwise. For here at last was the promised one, whose coming mankind had long awaited. Here indeed was the Saviour of the world, the Christ. Such was the discovery of that tiny village during two unforgettable days.

The departure from Sychar was a touching one with so many well-wishers seeing them off and so many entreaties to return that way again. The disciples had never suspected that Samaritans could feel so warmly toward a little band of Jews. More than that, they had never suspected the warmth that could be born in their own hearts toward members of so despised a race. They actually would not mind coming back to Sychar some day.

Up the northward road they went now, the peaks of Gerizim and Ebal gradually receding into the background as they made their way past row upon row of waving grain. Yes, they noted, those fields certainly were white for harvesting, just as Sychar had been in a sense much more deep and real. Could they, in fact, ever again look at nature's harvest, without recalling the harvest of God? They doubted it. And so, absorbed with such thoughts, they rapidly left that memorable little village behind.

In due course their journey had led them into Galilee, native soil both for them and for their Master. True, He at least had not actually been born there, though this fact was not generally known, but He had been reared in the village of Nazareth and now made His home in the lakeside town of Capernaum (Mt 4:13; Jn 2:12). Both Nazareth and Capernaum were Galilean cities, as was also Cana which they now, at length, approached.

They were surprised, when they crossed into Galilee, by the cordiality of the Galileans toward their teacher. They had observed well that He received no honor in His own country. In Nazareth, especially, He had been held in no special esteem. Trained at home in the trade of a carpenter, without formal theological instruction, He had never seemed to the villagers of Nazareth to deserve recognition as a qualified rabbi, much less as a prophet of God. After all, He was simply a well-known, hometown product, a young man barely thirty, whose claims to fame rested on no special achievements in the city where He grew up (Mk 6:1-6; Lk 3:23; 4:16-24; Jn 7:15). But this spirit, which to a greater or less extent pervaded the whole Galilean attitude toward Jesus, now seemed to be sharply diminished, and in its place there was a new-found atmosphere of respect.

The reason for this was not hard to find. As was their custom, the Galileans had recently fulfilled their religious obligations by going south to Jerusalem for Passover. Jesus, of course, had been there too and had astounded the many Jewish pilgrims who thronged that city by the miracles He had performed. The Galileans, therefore, had had opportunity at that feast to observe these miracles, and they were duly impressed. Now they were welcoming Jesus as the miracle-worker that He was.

But alas! He was more than that. He was a prophet who spoke the Word of God. Above all, He was the Christ whose word could create an inexhaustible well of life in every heart that trusted Him. This, at least, the Samaritans had learned simply by listening to Him talk. The Galileans had not learned it even by seeing the miracles He did. But those very miracles were now conditioning some of them for just such a realization as that.

They were entering Cana now and making their way toward the marketplace to buy supplies. The welcome here seemed unusually warm, and well it might have been. For this was the city where the Saviour had performed one of His most striking deeds of power. Six large waterpots of stone had been filled with water at the instructions of Jesus, while the festivities of a local marriage had swirled around them. Then the servants who had filled them (the pots altogether held nearly 120 gallons!) had been told to dip smaller vessels into these waterjars and to carry what they drew out to the master of ceremonies. But what they drew out was superbly tasty wine, which abundantly supplied the embarrassing lack of it which the wedding hosts had suddenly encountered (Jn 2:1-11). Thus, it was nothing less than the power of the Creator that Jesus had displayed in this city.

Of course, at first only the servants who had drawn the water were privy to the secret of its transformation. But in the days that followed they talked and talked about what their eyes had seen. Naturally they were not always believed, but now their report seemed to be confirmed by the miracles the Galileans had recently witnessed in Jerusalem. Cana, therefore, was like an open city to this traveler and to the group of men who followed Him.

Suddenly, through the crowd that was rapidly gathering around Jesus and His disciples, came a man whose costly-looking garments clearly marked him off from the rest of the villagers in Cana. The practiced eye could tell by a glance at the robe he wore that he belonged to the royal retinue which served in the court of Herod Antipas, the luxury-loving tetrarch of Galilee. As he approached Jesus, his drawn and haggard countenance betrayed alike the weariness of a journey and the deep anxiety within him. In a moment, he was before the Saviour pouring out the trouble which had brought him here.

He was indeed a courtier of Herod's, as his expensive clothing had revealed, and his home was the village of Capernaum on the shores of lake Gennesaret, to which Jesus not long ago had moved. There in Capernaum at this very moment his son lay desperately sick, and the father was full of fear that death was imminent. So, as soon as word had reached him that Jesus had returned from Judea and had entered Galilee, this nobleman had set out hoping to encounter Him on His northward route. How rapidly Jesus might travel through Galilee, or when He might intend to be in Capernaum, the father had had no way of knowing. But now he implored Him, without delay, to commence His journey there. Though the entire journey of some twenty miles could not be consummated that day, yet they might still make a start. Haste seemed urgently called for, and the courtier's pleas for this were plaintively insistent.

Jesus' answer startled him and sounded at first like a cold rebuff. "Unless you people see signs and wonders, you just won't believe."

It was true, of course. These Galileans were not like the Samaritans at all. The word of Jesus—unadorned by any visible display of the miraculous—did not seem to be sufficient for them. In Sychar it had been enough, but not here. A prophet—speaking simply as a prophet—had no honor in his own country.

"Sir, come down before my child dies." He almost wept the words. This man had the power to help him, he knew. How could He withhold it? The father could not bear to think of the tragedy that would follow.

The next words he heard were more startling than the first. "Go on back. Your son lives!" said Jesus.

My son lives? the nobleman thought. Then recovery was guaranteed. His boy would turn back from death's door. Wonderful promise! Could he believe it? Yes—yes, he could! He had no proof, there was nothing visible to rely upon, just the naked word of Jesus. That was all he had. But there was a solemnity in that word. The one who spoke it spoke in tones of absolute, unwavering authority. "Your son lives!" Believe it? Yes, he could—and he did!

Jesus and His disciples remained that night in Cana. The

nobleman did not. The journey which, just a short time before, he had insisted that Jesus make, he now made alone. Back to the north and east he went, across the Galilean hills, as far as he was able to go until night interrupted his travels. Early the next morning, at daylight, he arose, and soon he was once again on his way. But it was not long before he observed some travelers, on the same road, moving rapidly toward him from the opposite direction. The nearer they came, the more familiar they looked, until at length he could recognize in them his own servants. It was evident that they had news; nothing else could have brought them out. As soon as they met him they wasted not a moment in telling it.

"Your boy lives!" they announced to him. The words left him momentarily shaken. They were nearly identical to the words that Jesus Himself had spoken the evening before. At least, the crucial word was there—he *lives!*

Recovering his composure, the nobleman thought of a question. Perhaps, after all, the whole affair was simply one supreme coincidence. Perhaps, when he had left, his boy had begun to get better by himself. In that case the trip to see Jesus had been needless, and the words "Your son lives" had not had the decisive effect he at first imagined. There was one way to find out. He would ask these servants what time it had been when his son began to get better. Obviously, the answer to that question was crucial to him and would determine his whole view of what had transpired. So he posed it.

The reply was a bolt of lightning. "Yesterday, at the seventh hour, the fever left him," they reported.

The fever *left* him? Why then, it was not at all a matter of *beginning* to get better, but instead, of getting well all at once. Jesus had said to him, "Your son lives," but he had grossly underestimated those words! They were *not,* as he had originally believed, the point at which recovery commenced. That would have been wonderful enough, and it was all he had at first been capable of accepting. But they were more than that!

They were the point at which health had been restored completely. Those words started no process; they accomplished the whole work. They had healed his boy completely and instantaneously!

"Your son lives!" There was *life* in that utterance, and the nobleman could not now resist the next conclusion. A person who could speak those words with such a result, unhindered by the hills and valleys which separated Him from the one about whom He spoke them, must be more than a mortal man. After all, had it not been the *word* of the Creator-God that had caused all things to leap from nothingness into being? Did not the psalmist say of old, "By the word of the LORD were the heavens made; and all the host of them by the breath of his mouth. . . . For he spake, and it was done; he commanded, and it stood fast" (Ps 33:6, 9). The question that now framed itself in the nobleman's soul was no different than that which the woman at the well had posed to the villagers of Sychar. "Is this perhaps the Christ?" And the answer which his heart gave to it was identical to the woman's own: the nobleman believed.

In Cana of Galilee, Jesus made the water wine—the Maker's power had transformed one element of His creation into another! How appropriate that here too those words, "Your son lives," should transform sickness into health, imminent death into continuing life. But this was not all those words had accomplished in their creative potency. For by their means, Herod's courtier had been brought to believe that the One who uttered them was the Christ of God. And in the moment when that faith was born, an even greater act of creation transpired. For then and there, there sprang into being in the heart of the nobleman an eternal fountain, "a spring of water gushing up into eternal life." The *father* lived as well!

So the nobleman became God's workmanship, specially formed for particular good works. And for him too, as also for the woman of Sychar, those works began in a harvest field near at hand. In his case, the harvest field was found in his own home in the village of Capernaum. For no sooner did he arrive there than he reported to his entire household—servants and family alike—the discovery he had made about Jesus. His testimony was compelling, his conviction transparent, and fruit was gathered into eternal life. Everyone under his roof now agreed with him. This man called Jesus was indeed the Christ, the Saviour of the world.

Thus, from Samaria to Galilee, from Sychar to Capernaum, the power of Jesus' word was still the same. It created life in every believing heart. True, in Galilee the desire to see miracles had furnished at first a barrier to that creative work, while in Samaria it had not. But even in Galilee there was now one household at least where that word had won its total victory.

An entire family—that of the nobleman—now believed. But a tragedy remained. For in the very city where the nobleman lived, Capernaum, Jesus' own family had also recently come to live. And in *that* household His quickening word was still resisted. By an incomparable irony, some who had dwelt for years under the same roof with the Prince of Life knew nothing of that life nor of the power of His word which could impart it. Yet there was hope. For if the Creator's life-giving utterance had opened springs of living water within His own city, might it not also open them in like manner within the circle of His own family?

5

Born from Above

James 1:1-18

> *Do not err, my beloved brethren. Every good gift and every perfect gift is from above, and cometh down from the Father of lights, with whom is no variableness, neither shadow of turning. Of his own will begat he us with the word of truth, that we should be a kind of firstfruits of his creatures* (Ja 1:16-18).

"A prophet has no honor in his own country," had been the testimony of Jesus, and it was amply verified by the Galilean craving for miraculous proofs. Later the Saviour was to elaborate that testimony in an even more pointed way. "A prophet is not without honor, except in his own country, and among his own relatives, *and in his own house!*" (Mark 6:4). It was in His own house that the Son of God had tasted most deeply the bitter dregs of rejection and unbelief.

Jesus was the oldest of five brothers (Mk 6:3). Half-brothers, perhaps they should have been called, for though they were sons of the carpenter, Joseph, and his wife, Mary, He was the son of Mary alone, conceived by the power of God while she was yet a virgin (Lk 1:27-35).

It had not been easy, of course, for Joseph to adjust to the discovery that the woman betrothed to him was pregnant before their marriage was consummated. The explanation she gave, that the Spirit of God had produced this pregnancy, was more than he could accept. Indeed, he had made up his mind to formally annul their engagement with a minimum of public embarrassment to her, when his plans were interrupted by a divinely given dream. Reassured by this dream, Joseph went ahead with the marriage though he carefully refrained from fulfilling his physical desire until after the birth of Jesus (Mt 1: 18-25). Subsequently, however, their union became complete; and they had the joy of bringing sons and daughters into the world.

The four boys whom they bore were named James and Joses and Jude and Simon (Mt 13:55). James was the oldest; and as he grew to manhood, he soon displayed striking qualities of character and mind for leadership.

It was inevitable that questions about the birth of Jesus should linger on in the tiny village of Nazareth for many years. Apparently, the rumor circulated far beyond that little town once Jesus had become well known. Even in Jerusalem it was such common knowledge that, in a moment of controversy, the Saviour had to hear the cutting words, *"We* were not born out of fornication!" (Jn 8:41).

It was, therefore, quite unavoidable that Jesus' four brothers should hear what the townspeople sometimes said about His birth. Without doubt, they vehemently denied it and were ready to argue with anyone who cast aspersions on their mother. Still, they could not deny that in subtle ways both of their parents treated Jesus differently. Worse yet, they sensed that Jesus on His part regarded Himself as in some way different from them. They had to acknowledge that His conduct toward them was always exemplary and His attitude one of utmost graciousness. Still, there was something about Him they resented; and the fires of this resentment were periodically stoked by the ugly gossip in their village.

The situation worsened when Jesus began to preach. The irritation He aroused in them became greater than ever. At times it seemed to them He was almost prepared to admit the truth of those sordid speculations about His ancestry with

which they had had to contend. Only *He* made a virtue out of
it! For now, people had begun to speculate about their brother
in terms of the nation's Messianic expectations. And, both
implicitly and explicitly, Jesus seemed to encourage such spec-
ulation, and worse, to encourage the conclusion toward which
it pointed. But that was to claim to be the Son of God! How
could He trade so crassly on the shadows that still hovered
over His birth, as though to suggest that He had no merely
mortal origin but had come down from above! Who did He
think He was? After all, they grew up with Him!

None of the brothers felt these things more deeply than
James. After all, the rights of firstbirth were his if Jesus was
actually illegitimate. But he tried never to dwell consciously on
this thought, though at times it was difficult to suppress. And
then, when Jesus began to perform miracles, as His fame
spread and His popularity grew, the tension inside of James
seemed to rise also. Whenever he thought about his brother,
and the things his brother did and said, it was as if a storm
had arisen in his soul. He knew about storms, in particular the
sudden squalls that so often and so unexpectedly churned the
sea of Galilee into a frothing fury. And that was what his
heart was like at times. Who *was* his brother really? An im-
poster? A man gone out of his mind? (Mk 3:21). Or, was
He really what not a few had already come to believe—the
Son of God? How deeply James yearned for the wisdom that
would answer this question!

It was now hard for James and his brothers to get along with
Him. Whenever He came home, the tension between them was
electric. They rejected His claims, but at the same time they
prodded Him to prove them. "If You do these things," they
said on one occasion, "show Yourself to the world" (Jn 7:3-5).
"Give the world a spectacular and decisive demonstration of
Your claims," they were saying. "Settle the question once and
for all." It was a taunt, but it was also a cry for help. Deep in
their souls, *they* wanted to be sure!

And then tragedy came. For while they were in Jerusalem at one of the annual Passover celebrations, their brother's career was abruptly brought to a ruinous end. Unfortunately for Him, He had aroused the jealousy and enmity of the religious aristocracy in that city; and, conspiring with one of his own professed disciples, the leaders had managed both to arrest Him and to bring Him under an indictment of death.

The Roman mode of execution, crucifixion on a wooden gibbet, was horribly painful they knew; and they were not so far past brotherly feeling as to be unmoved by that.

Worst of all was the agony they knew their mother must pass through because of this. It would be like a sharp sword piercing her very soul, bringing an anguish such as only a mother can feel. Indeed, from a distance, they watched her standing desolate beneath Jesus' cross, with one of His most loyal disciples standing beside her (Lk 2:35; Jn 19:26-27).

They did not know till later that Jesus had committed the care of His mother to that disciple. Not to them, His brothers! But to a disciple. That touched them too, as though their eldest brother felt nearer to this follower of His than to them. But, of course, they understood why. After all, they had made their rejection plain to Him. They could not resent this dying act of His. It did, however, prick their hearts.

That happened on a Friday. On the Sunday that followed it, a discovery was made that was to shake the entire city of Jerusalem. The tomb of Jesus was found empty, and the report began to circulate in the ensuing days that some of His followers had seen Him alive. Naturally, the rumor reached Jesus' family and it astounded them. Mary seemed ready to believe it at once; that was quite natural, of course, for a mother, the brothers thought. But *they* were skeptical; not as before, however, with the skepticism that is born of hostility. Their feelings now were different, tinged with sorrow and a hope they dared not hope. If their brother *could* rise from the dead, then that would settle all their questions. Then they would have no trouble concluding— But that was foolish. They had seen Him die.

Then it happened! James saw Him (1 Co 15:7). Face to face they met and talked. And from that moment on, James, followed shortly by the other brothers as well, became a loyal and devoted bondslave of the very one who had grown up with him in the home at Nazareth (Ac 1:14).

James never denied their earthly brotherhood, but neither did he ever stress it. For now the relationship had been drastically transformed, and his brother was also his Lord. Now, too, he understood the mystery of Jesus' birth as he learned from his mother the miracle that had been wrought in the days of her virginity. It was that miracle which made possible the most momentous of all events—God became a man and lived on earth. His brother, therefore, was the Lord of glory. He had come down from the Father of lights above!

"James, a bondslave of God and of the Lord Jesus Christ" were the words that opened a pastoral letter he wrote years later. Much had happened in those years. The Christian church had been founded at Jerusalem, and many of its members had then been scattered by persecution throughout the regions of Judea and Samaria (Ac 8:1). James himself had risen to the place of leadership in the Jerusalem congregation, for which his basic instincts so aptly fitted him (Ac 15:13-21).

More than that, it seemed to those early Christian believers that James was very much like the brother he now called Lord. There was a moral integrity in James, coupled with a practical wisdom, that were unmistakably familiar to many who had seen and listened to Jesus. There was also a spirit of compassion, especially expressed in sympathy for the poor, the orphaned, and the widowed, that had in like manner marked the Saviour (Ja 1:27). Moreover, the Christians valued those intimate glimpses of their Master which, from time to time, they managed to pry out of James. But as much as anything, they valued his rich conception of God as the unrivaled Giver.

Some of the Christians to whom he wrote his pastoral letter were among the ones who had been scattered by that early persecution. Since that time, in all too many ways, they and their fellow believers had been sorely tried both by their circumstances and by the opposition and enmity of men. So James wrote to encourage them and to urge them to profit fully from every trial that came their way.

"Count it all joy," James said, "when you fall into 'many-colored' testings." For, he went on to assure them, God will use that trouble—whatever its shade or hue—to supply you with the very thing you lack to make you a well-rounded Christian person. Suppose, for example, the trouble reveals your lack of wisdom. The solution is simple. "If any of you lacks wisdom, let him ask of God, who gives liberally to all, and does not reproach; and it shall be given to him. But let him ask in faith, debating nothing. For the one who debates is like a wave of the sea driven and tossed by the wind. Don't let that man suppose that he shall receive something from the Lord."

"Be calm in your time of trouble," James was telling these Christians. "Quiet the storm in your soul, and let the waves of inward debate subside. Let there be a calm in your spirit, like the calm of a motionless sea, so that the voice of God may speak wisdom to your needy heart. You need only ask for it in faith. For He gives—oh, how liberally—and He never chides the ignorance which made it necessary to ask!" Had not James himself been ignorant once, his soul wracked by the violence of his inward uncertainty about Jesus? Yet that tempest had been stilled for him by a generous Lord who had granted the wisdom of faith. And now he was sure, therefore, that whatever lesser wisdom his readers might need would be bounteously bestowed by that same graciously giving God.

It was not long after these words were penned on the rough papyrus sheet before him that James returned again to the theme of giving. If the Christians to whom he wrote felt, in their time of trouble, some solicitation to do evil, let them never blame their temptation on God. The inclination to sin arose within themselves, he insisted, and the ultimate fruit of sin was death. Nothing like this, therefore, could originate with God. But what did originate with Him? The soul of James was now filled to overflowing as he dipped his pen and readied it to write the words that followed.

"Don't go astray, my beloved brothers." The words conveyed the tenderness of spirit with which he sought to instruct these fellow Christians, so dear to him. "Every good gift and every perfect gift is from above, coming down from the Father of lights."

It was a sweeping statement, much more than merely saying that if God gave a gift, it would be good and perfect. That was true, of course, but James meant something more. If a gift was good and perfect at all, then God had given it. "Every good gift and every perfect gift is from above." Man cannot give such gifts, compassed as he always is by the limitations and weaknesses of human nature, and every gift he gives will always have clinging to it some trace of his frailty, some hint of his own mortality. At their very best, man's gifts cannot last forever. At their very worst, they may be utterly unwise and unsuited for their intended recipients. No, if a gift were ever good and perfect in the truest sense of those words, it had to originate with God. It had to come down from above, from an unchanging Father of lights.

"Every good gift and every perfect gift is from above, coming down from the Father of lights, with whom there is no variation, neither any shadow cast by turning."

James was thinking now of those heavenly lights—the sun, the moon, the stars—of which God had become the Father by creating them. "O give thanks to the Lord of lords:" the psalmist of old had said, "To him that made great lights" (Ps 136:3, 7). Nevertheless, James was saying, the Creator is greater than His creation. The Father of lights is more wonderful than the lights themselves. For in Him there is not a trace of the variableness that is so clearly visible in the luminaries of heaven. The moon, that celestial orb that rules the night, passes regularly through its phases as it waxes and wanes from month to month. Similarly the sun, which rules the day, as it travels its appointed round from dawn to dusk, causes the shadows of earth to lengthen or contract according as it hangs low upon earth's horizon or blazes full-strength in the noonday sky.

All is change, nothing is without variation in the lights that illumine mankind. Not so with God. When He gives those good and perfect gifts, that He alone can give, they possess for all who take them the mark of their immutable Giver. As gifts they never fail to be all that a gift should be, the surpassing excellence that is theirs never fades or grows dim, and they never cast a shadow upon the life they bless.

When He gives, God is ever at the zenith of His glory, blazing forth like a noonday sun for which there can be no evening and no twilight. Good and perfect gifts He gives, and these alone—and these always. He is the Father of lights, "with whom there is no variation, neither any shadow cast by turning."

But how could James illustrate this truth? What gift shall he speak of, out of the countless gifts God gives, which could furnish the supreme demonstration of the principle he has just declared? The answer was obvious:

"Of His own will He begat us with the word of truth."

That was it! The gift par excellence! The very gift the Saviour had spoken of at Jacob's well, imparted by His word alone. The gift of life! God has given us *life,* James was saying, for He *begat* us. And the seed which brought that life into being was the seed of His own word. It was so because He *willed* it to be so. There was no effort on our part, no work, no labor; it was simply an act of the divine volition.

"Your son lives!" Such had been the utterance by which the life-imparting power of the Saviour's word had been displayed.

And though, during those long years of painful rejection, James had been a stranger to that power, he knew it now. The word of the gospel of God's Son, the word that declared eternal life to be freely available to man, that word, he knew, was the word of truth. And by means of it God could beget spiritual children, individual souls, like the woman at Sychar or James himself, who would then possess His very life.

"Of His own will He begat us with the word of truth, that we should be a kind of firstfruits of His creatures."

We are His workmanship, James thought, though the image he used to convey it was his own. The Father of lights, whose creative word had called the natural world into being, would someday remake that world so that all His "creatures"—every created thing—would be made anew. The Christian hope was clear and definite on this point. "We, in accordance with His promise, are looking for new heavens and a new earth, in which righteousness settles," an apostle was to say in the days ahead (2 Pe 3:13).

But Christians had looked for that new world from the very first. And James was looking for it too, and in doing so, pronouncing those whom God begot, to be the first tokens of its coming. We are a "kind of firstfruits" in relation to all creation, he affirms. What the first product of a season's harvest is to the harvest itself—like it in kind and a promise of more—such are we to the world to come. Remade by the vitalizing word of God, imbued with the life of the coming age, we are a foregleam of the new creation which is yet to be.

Could any gift be greater? Could any be more perfect? Clearly not. For this is eternal life. And as that life can never fail the one who has it, as it becomes within him a spring whose supply of water can never be exhausted, just so it is the gift best suited to display the unchanging character of Him with whom no variation is found, nor shadow cast by turning.

The Creator had walked on earth. In Cana He had turned the water into wine, and He had transformed the sickness of a little boy into exuberant health. Most amazing of all, it seemed to James, He had actually condescended to dwell in that home at Nazareth, an insignificant village of Galilee. The problem of His presence there had once caused a storm in the heart of James; but now that storm was stilled, and the wisdom of God was in its place. James knew now that this One had not originated in that home, but had come down from above. And with Him He had brought His most good and perfect gift— eternal life. Therefore, wherever He went, preaching and teaching (Oh, how it had once irritated James!), it was the word of truth He proclaimed and the gift of life He offered.

More than once James wished he could go back and relive those eventful years. Instead of staying behind at home, blinded by unbelief, he would have followed his heaven-sent brother about, and he would have hung on every vital word the Saviour uttered. How much he might have learned that way! How much the disciples who actually did follow Him about had learned! Indeed, it seemed to James that these disciples possessed so rich and varied an understanding of God's thoughts, that he could attend for hours upon end to the things they had heard in the company of Jesus. Now that James had been begotten by God's word of truth, he could never learn enough about the vitality of that truth in the hearts of those to whom it had given life. And it was precisely about this that the disciples seemed to be able to say so much. Naturally, therefore, when the disciples talked, James listened.

But James was far from complaining. Everything was according to God's sovereign plan. If he had never known what it was to follow the Son of God about as He proclaimed His word along the highways and byways of their native land, neither had the disciples known what it was to grow up with Him. How favored he had been! How unspeakably favored! To live under the same roof with the One who came down from heaven.

But there was one favor even greater than that! It was a

favor he shared now with the woman of Sychar, with the nobleman of Capernaum, and with the disciples themselves. And
on this subject he could speak every bit as eloquently as they.
Indeed, none of these ever described this favor with any greater
beauty than did James himself. "Every good gift and every
perfect gift is from above, coming down from the Father of
lights. Of His own will begat He us with the word of truth!"

6

The Seed of the Word

Luke 8:1-15

> *Now the parable is this: The seed is the word of God. Those by the way side are they that hear; then cometh the devil, and taketh away the word out of their hearts, lest they should believe and be saved. They on the rock are they, which, when they hear, receive the word with joy; and these have no root, which for a while believe, and in time of temptation fall away. And that which fell among thorns are they, which, when they have heard, go forth, and are choked with cares and riches and pleasures of this life, and bring no fruit to perfection. But that on good ground are they, which in an honest and good heart, having heard the word keep it, and bring forth fruit with patience* (Lk 8: 11-15).

"Of His own will begat He us with the word of truth." Thus had James identified the vehicle through which the gift of life was communicated to men. So, too, the villagers of Sychar had—in effect—confessed their indebtedness to that same word. "Now we believe," they insisted to the woman, "not because of your chatter; for we have *heard Him* ourselves, and know that this really is the Christ, the Saviour of the world."

The power of life, therefore, was resident in the words of Jesus, and His, "Your son lives," conveyed it on a physical plane in precisely the way His gospel did on the spiritual plane. His word, therefore, was like a seed, imparting the germ of eternal life to every believing heart.

James now knew the truth of the seedlike character of the Word of God, but he always regretted that he had not been present when the wondrous ramifications of that truth were first unfolded by the Son of God. That privilege had been granted to the disciples who had followed Him about while James stayed at home in his unbelief. Thus, in later years, James depended on these disciples to recount the simple but memorable narrative in which the Saviour had forever enshrined this truth.

And they could recount it well. Indeed, the parable of the seed and the soils had been indelibly etched on their minds and hearts, for of all the vivid stories the disciples had heard Jesus tell, there was none they had heard Him tell more often than this. Repeating it time and again as He did, their Master seemed also to signify thereby the importance He attached to it. Nor was He unwilling to explain more than once to them its inner meaning.

On one occasion in particular, they recalled in later years, they had been traveling with Him through numerous Palestinian villages and cities, followed by that loyal band of women who so faithfully served them in the mundane needs of their ordinary life. The journey they were taking with Jesus seemed to be attracting even greater crowds than usual. It appeared that every town and village through which they passed augmented the numbers who swarmed about them. The audience, therefore, was immense when Jesus paused one morning to teach.

The place He chose to stop was situated along a Galilean roadside. (It was quite impossible to accommodate so large a following inside a village or town.) In order that He might be visible to all to whom He spoke, their Master had chosen an elevated area dotted with rocks jutting sharply out of the ground, and on one of the stones atop this eminence He sat down.

It seemed fortunate to the disciples that at the base of this rise of ground there should be a tangled cluster of thorns, for this bramble thicket thus formed a natural barrier between Jesus and His audience, and furnished Him with much needed breathing room. In the road in front of Jesus, therefore, and in the farmer's field on its opposite side, the people followed His lead and began to sit down. When all had finally found a place which looked reasonably comfortable at least, the Saviour began to speak.

"A sower went out to sow his seed." The words sounded so natural in this agricultural setting, some of the crowd glanced instinctively at the field behind them, almost expecting to see a farmer engaged in his work.

"And as he sowed, some fell along the roadside, and it was trampled on and the birds of heaven ate it up." Now some of the people, who had managed to find a seat on the road just in front of Jesus, looked down. *Yes,* they thought, *the farmer who sowed the field beside us might easily have let some seed fall right here.* For when he reached his hand into the large sack that he carried suspended from his shoulder, and when he hurled a handful of seed across his land, not a few of those tiny grains might land on this very roadside. But here they could find no permanent lodging. They would soon be spied by the ever-present birds and be completely devoured by them. It was useless to look for any seed here now, or even any sprout. It had all long since been snatched away.

"And some fell upon a rock, and as soon as it had sprung up, it withered away, because it lacked moisture." *That too could easily happen right here,* the audience thought. If the farmer was near the roadside when he let fly a handful of seed, some of it might land across the road, right there on the rocky hillside where Jesus was sitting. Into the cracks and crevices of the stones which thrust their way above the surface of the ground, some of it might go, finding there a permanent home safe from the birds which so easily cleared off the roadside. But that was of little value to the farmer. Out of those cracks and crevices, the sprouts of would-be grain might soon appear, only to be withered and ruined by the heat to which they were then exposed. And because the seed could not penetrate its rocky home with roots capable of drawing moisture from the soil below, its fruit was doomed never to be produced.

"And some fell among thorns; and the thorns sprang up with it, and choked it." And, of course, the thorns were right there before their eyes. No one would have wished to thrust his hand into that jagged, tangled mass of brambles. What an uncongenial home they would make for a life-bearing grain of wheat! How could its shoots ever hope to emerge to maturity from that wretched environment? Surely, as Jesus said, they would be choked.

"And others fell on good ground, and sprang up and produced fruit one hundredfold." The point was clear. The fruitfulness of the seed depended on the character of the ground on which it fell. It was always the same seed, but not always the same soil. On the roadside, it lay exposed to the birds of heaven. On the rock, it could not penetrate its stony bed. In the thorns, it was crushed by the thicket which was its home. But on good ground, well-plowed and furrowed to receive it, the final crop could be marvelous indeed.

This much was clear. But the audience wondered why Jesus had told the story. So did the disciples. After all, its truths were self-evident in nature, and in a region dotted with farmlands its informational content seemed negligible indeed. Everyone, therefore, was a little surprised when Jesus moved on into a new line of teaching and offered no light at all on the parable He had told.

But a parable it was, the disciples were sure. They were familiar by this time with their Master's technique. And one of the best privileges of discipleship was the special information they often acquired from Him over and above what He disclosed to the crowds. So, at their earliest opportunity later that day, they asked for an explanation. "What might this parable mean?"

His reply revealed the reason for His reticence with the multitudes. "To you it has been granted," said Jesus, "to know the mysteries of the kingdom of God. But to the rest they are in parables, so that when they see they might not see, and when they hear they might not understand."

Their Master, they knew, did not regard God's truth as cheap or common. Neither did He feel that His audiences ought to have it cast before them without any challenge to their desire to penetrate its meaning. And this was especially true of anything which He regarded as a *mystery* of the kingdom of God. Indeed, when any of these divine secrets were expounded by Him, He always sought an audience deeply sympathetic to His instruction. Such an audience the disciples were, as were also the devoted women who followed Him. To them, but not to the fickle masses outside, the hidden realities which characterized God's kingdom were disclosed.

The Lord Jesus continued. "Now the parable is this: the seed is the Word of God."

Of course! What light that shed on the parable already, before anything else was said! The Word of God! The gospel of God's Son! This was the life-bearing seed of which He spoke—the word that had opened a spring of living water in hearts at Sychar and had done the same in their hearts as well. He was referring to the word of truth by means of which they were begotten to eternal life, as was also everyone who received that word in faith.

What marvelous potential for fruitage was latent in that word! Who could begin to estimate the capacity for good which it conveyed to the heart in which it found its lodging? Who could measure the fruit which it ought to produce for the glory of God? "We are His workmanship, created for good works," and those works ought to be as abundant as the vital source of life within could make them.

"Those by the roadside," Jesus explained, "are those who hear; then the devil comes and takes away the word out of their hearts, so that they won't believe and be saved."

That was clear enough, the disciples felt. There was a life-imparting power in God's Word which stirred the animosity of man's adversary. As surely as an effort was made to gain a home for that vital seed, by faith in some human heart, so surely would Satan seek to prevent it. Above all, he could not allow God's Word to lodge in that heart. He must somehow devour it, and thus remove it before faith occurred. For if faith occurred, so would salvation! It was a matter of urgency for him, "lest they should believe and be saved"!

In later years, if not at that moment, the disciples were also to consider the appropriateness of a roadside to describe the heart out of which the enemy retrieved God's Word. For a road, in contrast to a field or to ground containing rocks or thorns, was a thoroughfare for travel. The seed, Jesus had said, was "trampled on" and *then* the birds had snatched it away. And this suggested the kind of heart which was, so to speak, a roadway for many thoughts. Distracted, therefore, by its own concerns, its own ideas, its own ambitions, such a heart became a place where the Word of God was trodden down, smothered as it were, and crushed by the multiplied pre-occupations that made that heart their highway. Hence with his consummate skill and masterly insight into man's psychology, the devil could fan that heart into irrelevant or confused activity at the very moment it was hearing the word of truth. Thus the Word was not heard in faith, its simplicity not discerned or appreciated, and its bearing and relevance very shortly forgotten. And so the enemy had effectively snatched it away. Salvation did not take place.

Before Jesus had said anything else, however, one fact was intuitively obvious to the disciples about the rest of His parable. From the roadside—and from the roadside alone—the Word of God had been retrieved. By the Saviour's own ex-

plicit observation this retrieval was for the purpose that salvation might not occur. Here, but here alone, Satan had tri-
umphed completely. The birds had devoured the seed. But
from the rocky ground, from the ground with thorns, and from
the furrowed field, the vital seed had never been removed.
Whatever the fruit produced, whether none or much, the seed
had found its home in the soil into which it fell, and the ma-
lignant birds had never touched it.

The inference from this was plain. Into all of the remaining
hearts, whatever the character of their soil, new life had come.
The quickening seed, the living utterance of a living God who
of His own will begot men with the word of truth—it was this
that had fallen permanently into those hearts. But how different the results! The disciples waited eagerly for further light.

"Those on the rock are they who, when they hear, receive
the word with joy. And these have no root, who believe for
a while, and in time of testing turn away."

Yes, the disciples had been right. Faith *had* occurred in the
heart the Saviour now described, and not mere passive faith,
adequate though that would be, but *joyous* faith. "When they
hear, they receive the word *with joy.*" But alas! The faith by
which they appropriated the gift of life had not endured. These
were they "who for a while believe, and in time of testing turn
away."

The *faith* had not endured. God's *gift* had! Indeed, that
gift always endured, for "whoever takes a drink of the water
that I shall give him," Jesus had insisted, "will never thirst!
But the water that I shall give him shall become inside of him
a spring of water gushing up into eternal life."

Man, to be sure, was changeable. The God who gifted him
was not! And the gift of life, like every other good and perfect gift, had its origin and source in an immutable giver. It
came down from above, from the Father of lights with whom
there is no variation nor any shadow of turning. No, their

Master's meaning was plain. The living seed remained in the heart. The faith that received it did not.

Tragic fact! The disciples believed they had seen it in operation. They could even remember individuals in some of the many cities through which they passed, who had heard their Master's word with almost boundless enthusiasm. Openly and boldly they had acknowledged Him as God's Christ and rejoiced in the salvation they received from Him. So stirring, in fact, had been their initial response that others in their village had been aroused by it and brought to share their faith. Thus, with startling quickness, the living seed within them was shooting forth its sprouts.

Yet sadly, after a lapse of months, when next the Saviour passed that way, it had been hard to get in touch with these individuals. And when they were found, the coldness of their greeting, the averted eye, the transparent excuse to be going— all told the same somber tale. Their attitude had changed, their faith was gone. Often, when the disciples made inquiries in those places, there emerged a tangled web of circumstances prominently woven with the dark threads of trouble and persecution. The initial enthusiasm they had felt had collapsed under the burden of trials and testings. And with it, so had their faith.

But how helpful was their teacher's parable in understanding such cases. The ground in those hearts was *rocky* ground. The terrain on which the seed had fallen was hard, tough, and resistant. And for this very reason it was shallow as well, for the seed could not penetrate its stony barrier to send its roots deep into the moisture-laden soil. Hence, all the sooner it sprouted upward, but all the sooner too it withered away when exposed to the remorseless heat. Without the opportunity to probe the very depths of its home, the seed could produce no crop.

So now they understood! Henceforth they would not assume that initial enthusiasm was invariably a sign that the heart

was fertile. Indeed, it might indicate the very reverse, for it
might mark a shallowness of spirit through which the truth of
God could scarcely penetrate. Only time and testing could
reveal the sort of soil God's Word had found. Better, by far,
for the shoots to delay their appearance while the truth sent
roots deep into the soul it had entered, so that in the end the
fruit might be abundant and the presence of the seed unmistakably displayed.

For once the little sprigs upon the rocks had died, who
could guess that hidden within its cracks was a life-giving seed?
Who would suppose that a man who turned away from his
faith had ever had life at all? But if it had been there once, it
remained there still. And that was one of the mysteries of the
kingdom of God!

But what about the thorns? The Saviour continued. "Now
that which fell among thorns—they are the ones who have
heard and when they go their way are choked by cares and
riches and the pleasures of life and bring no fruit to maturity."

It was getting easier now. There was progression in the
Master's figures. The seed on the roadside vanished completely, never displaying its vitality at all by so much as a single
sprig. The seed on the rocks shot forth a few sprouts, evidence
of the life that produced them, but these were soon gone. But
the seed among thorns did better. The vital life that seed contained was working once again, but the stalk of grain it produced was stunted and never became fully ripe. The thorns
among which it found its home had stifled its maturation and
were dooming it to become a perpetual pygmy.

The disciples knew all too well the type of person to whom
the thorns applied. More than once, in their presence, Jesus
had invited some person to follow Him (Lk 9:59-62). That
person, perhaps, had newly come to believe in Him, and now
the Saviour was setting before him the pathway of discipleship.
Having bestowed on that heart the water of life, He now invited it to eat His food.

His call was a challenge to do the will of God and to finish His work. But all too often the invitation was politely declined. There were family responsibilities; there were business interests; life with Jesus would be too hard; there were a thousand excuses, but they all came down to the same things. The cares of life, the pleasures of life, the love of money—these then were the thorns! Searing, jagged thorns, deeply entrenched in the same heart into which the Word of God had come in life-bestowing power.

It was not a question of losing one's faith, as with those whose hearts were rocky ground, but a question of finding room for the truth of God to flourish. It was a question of allowing the life of God within to grow to its full expression, and to produce the luxuriant harvest of works for which the seed was sown. But the thorns prevented this, and grew up along with God's Word and choked it back.

Fortunately, the disciples thought, *there was another kind of soil.* "But that on the good ground," concluded Jesus, "they are the ones who, having heard with a heart that is honest and good, hold fast the Word and with endurance bring forth fruit."

The disciples could not help thinking of the women who traveled with them. Mary Magdalene was one of them; and Joanna, the wife of a responsible Herodian official named Chuza; and a woman called Susanna; and many others. What a help they had been in so many ways! They had cooked, they had sewed, they had expended time and energy and, by no means least, their own money—all that the Saviour's tours to preach God's Word might by their efforts be made a little more comfortable for Him.

Joanna, in particular, had left the comfortable life at the court of Herod Antipas, to follow Jesus on these grueling journeys. They had lost track of the money she had spent—probably she herself had lost track—for she was extremely well-to-do.

What made them different from others who heard God's

Word and believed it? Was it not the attitude of their hearts? Was it not the spirit of gratitude that imbued them? Surely they had hearts which, like a thoroughly furrowed field, were good soil on which God's seed had fallen! No wonder they persisted in following the Saviour month after month along the wearisome paths He trod!

The disciples marveled at the loyalty of the women, but they also understood it. Their own hearts furnished them an explanation they were confident they could apply to others. It seemed to them that devotion to the Saviour was the only sensible, honest course they had. After all, had He not granted to them that gift of life by which they could be assured a place with Him in the world to come? Were they not, by virtue of possessing that gift, forever preserved from the damnation of hell? It was a glorious gift, and one so good and perfect as to inspire, they felt, the utmost gratitude toward its giver. No task, therefore, was too large to do, no sacrifice too great to be made for Him. The women felt that way, too, the disciples believed.

There was not a trace in them of that hardness and shallowness of heart which, like stony ground, allowed God's truth to dwell only on the surface. Already the roots of the new life they had received had penetrated their souls most deeply, drawing up the moisture of devotedness and love to God.

Nor were they bothered by thorns. They could all have stayed at home, pleading the pressing concerns of daily living, but they had not done so. Would their fruit reach maturity? Would the harvest of their lives for God be truly abundant? The disciples felt confident they knew the answer. They could only wish their own hearts to be as honest and good as they believed these women's to be.

What insight they had gained from this simple parable! The seed was the Word of God! And only the heart from which it could be snatched at once, before it had been grasped by faith —only a heart like that would fail to partake of life. But the measure of life, the extent of its fullness and blessing, this depended on the kind of soil into which the seed had come.

It was always the same vital seed, vibrant with eternal life and all of the divine potential of that life. But if it could not put down deep roots into its new-found home, the evidences of its presence would be brief and passing, little more than a few weak shoots quickly withered in the heat of testing. And if it must grow on the same ground with a worldly spirit, with a love for money or for pleasure, or simply grow in a heart pervaded by earthly cares, it could never reach the real limits of its promise or attain the full stature toward which it strove.

No, the full harvest of good works in the life of one who had tasted the water of life depended on the heart's possessing a sincerity that could lay firm hold on God's Word and hold fast its truth as a most prized possession. It depended on a dedication of spirit capable of endurance under trial and testing. The life within the seed was the gift of God. But the fruit of that life depended on the spirit of the man in whose heart the seed now dwelt.

The disciples thought they had heard this before. In fact they were sure of it. One could freely take of the water of life and possess it forever. But one must labor to do the will of God and to finish His work. And unless a man did, that might always remain food which he knew not of!

7

Discipleship:
Saving the Life We Lose

Luke 9:18-26

And he said to them all, If any man will come after me, let him deny himself, and take up his cross daily, and follow me. For whosoever will save his life shall lose it: but whosoever will lose his life for my sake, the same shall save it. For what is a man advantaged, if he gain the whole world, and lose himself, or be cast away? For whosoever shall be ashamed of me and of my words, of him shall the Son of man be ashamed, when he shall come in his own glory, and in his Father's, and of the holy angels (Lk 9:23-26).

Following the Lord Jesus around through the towns and villages of Palestine could be very exhausting. Sometimes the disciples were almost tempted to ask if it was really worth it all. Occasionally, in some rare moment when they could escape the crowds, they would simply sit in silence each thinking his own thoughts. And in those times of reflection, it was natural that their minds should wander back to home and family and friends.

It almost seemed that life was passing them by. Instead of traveling these dusty highways, trying to communicate with mobs of people who often seemed so unappreciative and uncomprehending, they should be back with their wives, earning a solid living, and rearing their children. That was what everybody else seemed to be doing, even many who believed in their

Master and had accepted His gift of life. And if others, why not them? As things were now, they sometimes thought, they were losing their lives. In the very prime of their years, they were missing out on life's basic satisfactions.

Such reflections, however, were usually very fleeting. They knew why they were doing what they did. The Saviour in whom they so deeply believed had called them to this life. Had He been just another man they would have left Him in a moment. But He was more than a man, more indeed than the greatest of men, more than the greatest spokesmen for God in Jewish history. He was the world's Redeemer. That's why they followed Him. Let others' hearts be stony ground. Let others be choked by the thorns of worldly cares. *They* would follow Jesus.

Some of them glanced in His direction. He was praying. There were few things that moved them more than seeing Jesus pray. That was a side of Him the crowds never saw. For when Jesus wanted to pray, He always tried to get away from the multitudes who thronged Him. But He didn't mind having *them* around and how glad they were He didn't. They had never seen anyone pray like He did. His words were not usually audible to them, His habit being to go off from them a little distance. But they didn't need to hear the words. It was evident that, for Jesus, prayer was the richest form of communion with His heavenly Father that anyone could imagine. They watched His face, if they could, and, if they were close enough, His eyes, upturned toward heaven. What simplicity of spirit (they thought they could detect), what trust, what love! They wished *they* could pray like that. Perhaps He would be willing to teach them someday (Lk 11:1).

He was finished now; and, rising from His knees, He walked back toward them. His face was thoughtful as He sat down with them, and presently He posed a question.

"Whom do the people say that I am?" He asked.

There was no single answer to that question. The disciples

had heard many conjectures as they had mingled with Jesus' audiences. Most people, indeed, agreed that Jesus was someone of great importance in the plan of God. But here the consensus ended, and diversity of opinion began.

"John the Baptist," they began, offering a highly popular suggestion, "but others say Elijah, and others that one of the prophets of old has arisen again."

"And whom do *you* say that I am?" Jesus continued.

Of course, He knew already who they thought He was. But, as was often His custom, He preferred to draw the assertion from them rather than simply to make it himself. Master instructor that He was, He knew full well that a truth clearly stated once by a pupil was worth ten such statements from His teacher.

And their answer *was* clear, as it was also most emphatic. Peter spoke it for the rest. "The Christ of God," he asserted.

It was a crucial affirmation. Had Jesus been simply some reappearing prophet of old, or John the Baptist recently beheaded but now returned to life, or even Elijah come back from the heavens into which he had been miraculously taken, that would have been a marvelous thing. And the crowds were prepared to believe that something marvelous was taking place in those days. But there was no salvation in such conjectures. Even the greatest of prophets could not give the gift of eternal life. The woman of Sychar had learned that. No, to give men living water, Jesus must be who the disciples said He was, the Christ of God.

They were surprised by the reaction that Peter's confession drew from their Master. For no sooner was it made, than He began to charge them quite sternly to tell no man this fact. They understood, of course, what He meant; He wished them to do precisely what He had just done to them. The truth about His person was something they should seek to elicit from men, as a conclusion of their own, rather than a fact to be forced on them by direct assertion. This had been the Saviour's method from the first.

At Jacob's well for example, He had not mentioned His Messianic title until first it had been mentioned by the woman. "I know," she had said, "that Messiah is coming, the one who is called the Christ. When He has come, He will tell us all things." That, of course, was the conclusion He had wanted her to reach, and He was ready at once to confirm it. "I, the one who is speaking to you, am He," He had said. But it was *her* conclusion really, to which He had deftly led her by the insight and wisdom in His words. It was thus, too, that He frequently preferred to lead men, step by step, to faith and to salvation. In that respect, therefore, there was nothing particularly new in this stern command.

But it seemed to them that there was a new urgency in what He said. There was also a new reason.

"The Son of man," said Jesus, "must suffer many things and be rejected by the elders and chief priests and scribes, and be killed and rise again on the third day."

They found this hard to assimilate. As the Christ of God, they thought then, He must surely enter very soon upon a glorious reign in the kingdom He was destined to establish. It was only after the events He now described had actually transpired that the disciples came to understand how necessary they had been. He might indeed have founded His kingdom at once—no human power could have stood against Him had He chosen to do so—but it would have been a kingdom empty of men. Holy angels, of which there were myriads, could have entered that kingdom. But not guilty men made of flesh. The gift of eternal life itself, a gift which guaranteed men's access to that kingdom, could not have been given to any heart apart from the fateful events of which Jesus was now speaking.

A gift, of course, is free to one who receives it. But it may be immeasurably costly to its giver. And so it is with the gift of eternal life. Freely offered to any who might ask for it ("If

thou knewest the gift of God . . . thou wouldest have asked"),
it was nevertheless a benefaction for which a terrible price
was paid. And Jesus, its giver, must pay it. He must suffer, He
must die. He must bear the sins of those to whom He gave
His gift, yes, and even of those who to their eternal sorrow
rejected it.

This the disciples did not yet understand. But when they
did, they made it a part of the message they proclaimed to
men. Then they fully subscribed to the words yet to be uttered by another apostle named Paul, "how that Christ died
for our sins according to the scriptures; and that he was buried,
and that he rose again the third day according to the scriptures" (1 Co 15:1-4).

It was of these necessary events that Jesus now spoke to
them. "The Son of man *must* suffer many things," He was
saying, "and be killed, and be raised the third day." And the
necessity for this seemed to be the reason He now insisted on
a greater reticence on their part in divulging that He was "the
Christ of God." The blindness of the crowds, their misguided
guesses about who He was, would soon play into the hands of
Jesus' enemies. The elders of the nation, the chief priests of
the temple, the scribes of the Jewish law—all these hostile
forces would find that a blind and unbelieving mob was easy to
manipulate during the tragic events which lay ahead (Mt 27:
20-25). Though the disciples were only dimly aware of what
it all meant, from now on they were walking with Jesus in the
shadow of His cross.

Little wonder, therefore, they were later to think, that the
next time He spoke to all the people His words were shaped
by this new theme He had just introduced and about which
He had no doubt been praying.

"If any man wants to come after Me," the Saviour said to
all His hearers, "let him deny himself, and let him take up his
cross day by day and follow Me."

It was the first time He had mentioned the word "cross." To the audience at large the expression might seem scarcely intelligible. To the disciples, against the background of His private remarks to them, the word had powerful meaning. Clearly, it signified death. And such a death—slow, lingering, agonizing! The thought chilled them. Moreover, His words brought to life in their minds the familiar image of a convicted criminal carrying his own wooden gibbet to the spot chosen for his execution. Thus their Master was saying (they could hardly believe He was saying it!) that they, like an assortment of guilty malefactors, should take up their own cross and fall in line with Him! He had told them He must die. Now He was telling them to get in step behind Him!

Obviously, this was no way to attract disciples from that crowd. Indeed, it was a good way to repel them. Surely, when experience showed how many there often were whose hearts had rocky or thorny soil, this was no way to surmount the impediment which the living seed of God's Word encountered in such lives. But, on second thought, He probably knew that. Undoubtedly He did. It was not at all a question of appealing to the heart that was hard or worldly, but an effort to sort out from them all the heart that was honest and good. It was, therefore, an effort to shake down His following and to appeal only to those whose devotion was real.

It was all of a piece. His reluctance to force upon men the conclusion that He was "the Christ of God" when they were satisfied to think that He was only a prophet, and His reluctance to lure men into discipleship without the most stringent warning of its cost.

In the former case, the gift of the water of life would be missed by those who were content to remain in their blindness. In the latter case, the food of doing God's will would be missed by those who were content to remain in a life of ease. As the hour of His rejection approached, with all of its tragic sorrow for those who were nearest to Him, the Saviour was weeding out the unmotivated and the insincere.

Did He really mean for them *all* to die? Maybe, but that was by no means clear. It was evident to the disciples that there was a symbolic content in this utterance. They were to take up their cross *day by day*. Obviously, it was not a question of picking up a literal piece of wood and lugging it around each day. Their trips were wearisome enough as it was! No, it must rather be a matter of principle, a matter of accepting— on a daily basis—all that a cross might mean. And with this, He had coupled a call for self-denial.

Later, when they had more opportunity to reflect, they realized that this was what discipleship was all about. Whenever they dreamed of home, or loved ones, or of comforts left behind, yet persisted in following Jesus wherever He led them, this was the self-denial of which He spoke. And when each day seemed to them a day when their personal lives were lost in the interests of God's work and the spread of the gospel, this surely was a kind of dying in which they took up a cross *day by day*.

To follow Jesus, then, was to resign one's personal interests, to say no to the natural desire to realize one's full potential for earthly satisfaction, and to accept a cross in its place. It sounded rather stern when it was put that way. There was no mention of the deep joy that only those who tasted that splendid food of doing God's will could know. But that was their Master's purpose at this point. He was going to a cross, with all its stark reality and suffering. No one who truly wished to give their life to Him should be under any delusion that the way was soft and easy. Rewards, even here and now, there undoubtedly were in such a life. But there were deprivation and suffering, too—perhaps even death—and the true disciple should accept that premise *day by day*.

How fortunate that one's entrance into the kingdom of God did not depend on his discipleship. If it did, how few would ever enter that kingdom! Indeed, the disciples themselves could not help wondering if they could really measure up, in the long run, to such standards. If eternal life had depended on doing so, the disciples could have felt no assurance that they really possessed it or ever would. They could only have hoped that they might make it in the end.

But how sweet, how incomparably sweet, to know that life was truly theirs—right now—as the gift of God. They had not earned it, they could not lose it! They had drunk the living water and would never thirst for it again—forever! And they were amazed, when they pondered it, how this assurance actually undergirded and strengthened their determination to go on being disciples. They might have thought that it would do the reverse—that it would make them careless, knowing that their eternal destiny was secure. But it didn't at all. In fact, it gave to them that basic inner security in their relationship to Jesus which was their best protection against discouragement and failure.

Discipleship was hard and, if their Master's words meant anything, it was destined to get harder. It would have been psychologically intolerable if they had thought that failure somewhere down the road would destroy their whole experience with God. But it couldn't. Whatever lay ahead, exhilarating or depressing, the living spring within them would keep on gushing up into eternal life. And that thought was like a spiritual Gibraltar, against which the waves of self-doubt and discouragement could spend their force in vain.

The next words of Jesus were as solemn and sobering as the ones they had just heard. They also confirmed the impressions those previous ones had made on them.

"For whoever wants to save his life, will lose it. But whoever loses his life for My sake, this person will save it."

Yes, they had been quite right in interpreting those earlier words as they had done. The cross they must daily take up in order to follow Jesus spoke to them of losing their life. The

very life they so often felt they really *were* losing during endless days on the road with the Saviour. They still breathed
and ate and slept, of course. But in terms of earthly joy and
the realization of worldly ambitions, such an experience was a
gigantic zero. It was life minus all that men of the world call
"life." It was, therefore, in its essence the loss of "life."

Yet, Jesus was saying, when men try to preserve their lives
they actually end up losing them. And when they lost them
for Him, as the disciples were doing day by day, they were
really saving them. It was a striking paradox. And though it
required much more thought than the disciples could give it
just then, its general significance was clear. It would be easy
enough for a man to decline the rigors and deprivations of discipleship in order to cling to his home, family, business, and
pleasures. It was natural to want to live one's life here and
now to the full, but to do so was to sacrifice its eternal value.
Living like that was selfish living and could really have no enduring significance or worth. Such a life was gone as soon as
it was lived. Thus in seeking to preserve it, a man actually lost
it.

Conversely, the Master's paradox asserted, to lose one's life
for His sake was, in fact, to save it. To find therefore in Jesus
a focus for living, which superficially seemed to sacrifice so
much that men hold dear, was to discover the secret of extending the value of that life into an eternal future. The disciples
were not so obtuse to the spiritual realities which their teacher
proclaimed that they could not sense the truth of this.

Take only the basic matter of offering the water of life to
thirsty sinners. There, beyond a doubt, was an activity fraught
with timeless consequences. To labor in God's harvest fields,
to do His will and to finish His work, this was, they had learned,
a process by which fruit was gathered in to eternal life. However hard and frustrating these preaching tours with Jesus
might seem at times, one immutable fact remained; God's barn
was being filled with sinners saved by grace. And as reapers,

the disciples knew, when the entire harvest was finally in, their joy would be immense. Then, indeed, they could look back over their lives from the vantage point of God's future kingdom, and they could be satisfied that those lives had been well spent. In that day, they could look around them at the men and women they had helped to reach and win, and they could know that their temporal experience of human life had not been wasted or annulled by selfish and self-serving pursuits. The life they thought they had lost for Jesus had in fact been saved. Their self-denial in the present would be more than compensated for by their joy and fulfillment in the future.

Of course, there was also the possibility of actual loss of life in the service of God. By His own admission, their Master was heading for just such an experience. And, of course, the words He spoke would be fully as true in that case as they were on any other level of meaning.

If a man sought to preserve his physical life, when the service of God called on him to lay it down, such self-preservation would involve incalculable loss. On the other hand, to literally die for Jesus' sake was to enhance supremely the eternal worth of the life thus surrendered for God.

The principle was always the same. Selfishness sought to protect life for one's own use and gratification. Discipleship yielded it up—if need be, in the ultimate sense of that idea—for the accomplishment of God's will and work. The former way in the light of an eternal future was to lose one's life. The latter way was the saving thereof. But it was not a once-for-all sacrifice of which the Master spoke, except in the final act of martyrdom itself, but a daily submission to the principle of self-giving, for the glory of God. "Let him take up his cross *day by day,*" Jesus had said, "and follow Me!"

The Saviour continued to speak. "For what is a man profited, if he gains the whole world, but loses [forfeits] himself?"

The world of commerce was now before their teacher's mind. The balance sheets were being totaled. Suppose, on the positive side of life's ledger, one could set down the entire world as a gain. This would be selfishness magnified to the nth power. All that man could wish or hope for in life, the world's pleasures and possessions without the subtraction of a single jot or tittle—all this fully experienced and enjoyed during his days on earth. What a "profit," it might seem, such a life should show.

Not so, said Jesus. For on the negative side of the same ledger, one must enter "my self." In the process of gaining all that the world had to offer, the price for this was a man's own self, which he had thoughtlessly cast away and lost. It would be a massive forfeiture, indeed. So massive, in fact, that when measured against the gain recorded in the opposite column, the total profit would stand at zero. "For what is a man profited. . .?" the Saviour had asked. And the answer was obvious—absolutely nothing!

When the present world, with all its potential for enjoyment and material gain, had passed away, the man who had realized that potential to the limit would have nothing left. Naked he had come into the world, and naked he would leave it again. For nothing that he had selfishly experienced or acquired in that world could be extended into the kingdom of God. The age to come would obliterate the fulfillments of earth-bound living as completely as a new day obliterates the nighttime that precedes it.

Nothing in a man's present human experience, therefore, is eternal, except the man himself. Thus it is imperative that a man cultivate *himself,* rather than the world in which he lives! It is indispensable that he learn the lessons of life, and enter into its most precious secrets, if he wishes to become a fully developed personality, prepared to enjoy the kingdom of God. And only thus would his life show a genuine and enduring "profit."

Not all of the ramifications of their Saviour's thoughts were evident just now to the disciples. Later they were able to penetrate them more deeply. And when they did, they realized that the premise of all which He now uttered was a simple one—suffering and self-sacrifice are what truly make a man. The man who lives an easy, self-indulgent life is a hollow shell, too weak to resist the slightest pressure, too unworthy to deserve the slightest honor. Years later, one of the disciples, Peter by name, was to write glowingly of the significance of suffering in the lives of the followers of Jesus. "May the God of all grace," he was to say to his fellow-Christians, "who has called you to His eternal glory in Christ Jesus, *after you have suffered a little,* make you complete—He will confirm, strengthen, settle you" (1 Pe 5:10). God, therefore, said Peter, desires to mold you in the crucible of affliction, and thereby to make you all you ought to be. "May the God of all grace make you *complete.*"

The "complete" man, the fully-developed person, that was what the Master was training those who followed Him to become. It requires self-denial, it requires the daily acceptance of a cross, it entails coming to know what it means to lose life in order to save it—but it is profitable! Selfhood, fully realized in all its grand potential for the age to come—this was what He offered. Over against it stands the whole world, and men must choose. They cannot have both. If you gain one, you lose the other. And in truth "what *is* a man profited, if he gain the whole world, but loses [or forfeits] *himself*"!

What does it mean for the future if a man really does forfeit himself? What, in particular, does it mean for one who has accepted the gift of life? What lies in store for those whose hearts prove to be rocky ground, or full of thorns? The next words of Jesus cast a flood of light upon it all.

"For whoever shall be ashamed of Me and of My words," the Lord Jesus now affirmed, "of him the Son of man shall be ashamed, when He shall come in His own glory, and in His Father's, and in that of the holy angels."

It was a splendid panorama that their Master had opened up

before them, a scene filled with light and wonder, the day of
His coming to reign. Though they did not yet clearly perceive
that He must go away, they sensed from His words that somehow He would appear to men in that day with a glory which
was now veiled from their eyes. It was, of course, the kingdom
of God, the kingdom about which they dreamed and for which
they longed. All the glorious angels of God would be there
amidst the splendor as well, and the brilliant effulgence of
the Father Himself.

No unquickened mortal, they realized instinctively, could
stand in that awesome light. No mere human being could
enter that luminous realm, unless they had been divinely prepared for it. Indeed, the disciples knew that the Saviour had
said, "Except a man be born again, he cannot see the kingdom
of God" (Jn 3:3). And they knew it was true. Unless the
Father of lights, from whom proceeded every good and perfect
gift, should of His own will beget a man with the word of
truth, that man must be banished forever from the divine presence and from the glory of the divine kingdom. But if He
begot them, then they became a sort of firstfruits of all His
creatures, ready ahead of time for the new age which was someday to dawn. The gift of eternal life, therefore, must be possessed by all who would find a place in that radiant, iridescent
scene.

But some *were* there of whom *He* was ashamed! He said
nothing of casting them out, nothing of banishing them from
Him, only that He was ashamed of them, amidst the splendor
all around. If they were there, they had to possess the gift of
life. But there was something they now tragically failed to
possess. For it was clear that they lacked the worthiness of
character which would have made Him proud to acknowledge
them. In a day when He Himself was so highly honored, He
could not honor them at all.

Why was He ashamed of them? Because *they* had been
ashamed of *Him!* Not that they rejected Him, not that they

did not believe, it was simply that He was an embarrassment to them. Instead of exhibiting the loyalty of true discipleship, instead of picking up their cross of self-denial day by day and clearly walking before men as followers of Him, they had been ashamed to do so. They were ashamed of Him personally, and—equally sad—ashamed of His words.

Thus, the life-giving message that had reached them had not been vigorously spread by them. Into the harvest fields of God they had not entered unreservedly, to gather fruit to life eternal. While others, like the women, for example, followed Him faithfully about, if only they might in some measure make Him a little more comfortable as He preached God's Word, *they* had stayed at home. To bear a cross behind Him had been to them a scandal, not an honor. And whether the soil of their hearts had been stony or marred by thorns, they had still failed dismally and disastrously to become worthy of His praise in the presence of His Father and in the presence of His holy angels.

So that was what it meant to lose oneself! It was the utter forfeiture of personal merit and worth in the very moment when it counted most. For now, in that day, no longer did the tinseled sham of a temporal world delude the eye or beguile the heart. No longer could the unworthy among men be exalted, while the worthy were disdained. Reality had now banished mere pretense, and devastating truth shattered men's miserable hypocrisy. Now, at last, if the life a man had lived had *really* mattered, the universe was ready to behold it. The holy angels were there to observe, the Father was prepared to approve, but *Jesus* must commend! And if He could not, if He would not—that was the ultimate personal shame. Indeed, if a man had possessed all the world right up to that very instant of time, it would have mattered no more. For all that mattered now was what he was, the man himself, in the eyes of his eternal Maker and Redeemer.

"For what is a man profited, if he gains the whole world,

but loses [forfeits] himself?" The divine accounting said
"zero," and eternity would verify that total. For if the man
himself was nothing, having lived for self and not for God, his
possessions amounted to nothing as well. For *they* would then
be gone, and *he* alone would remain. The question about life,
therefore, which the Son of God was addressing to His hearers
was profoundly searching. It was not, "What did you *have?*"
but, "What did you *become?*" And if a man *became* a true
disciple to the Master, he would be acknowledged and honored
in the kingdom of God. And if not, the Saviour would be
ashamed.

It seemed to the disciples that, when they considered it, they
were almost overwhelmed by the solemnity of such thoughts.
Rugged as their itinerant experience with Jesus often was, to
glimpse reality in this light was to gain from it a new measure
of purpose and determination. No longer could they envy
those who, though believing in their Master, had shunned the
pathway to which He invited them in order to avoid the hardships which it entailed. Indeed, they could only pity them and
feel a touch of sorrow at the shame which one day awaited
these who had chosen their course so poorly.

In later years it was to be the disciples' privilege to teach
such precepts to many in the fledgling Christian church. Men
like James who had not even been believers during the Saviour's career on earth would be deeply challenged and profoundly motivated by these truths. The conscience of Jesus'
followers was to be permanently colored by this very wisdom
that the disciples were gleaning along the dusty roads of Galilee and Judea. Of course, just now, the disciples could not sense
how richly profitable their growing insight would be to believers in all future time. But for the moment they could sense
how richly profitable it could be for them! Indeed they made
up their minds they would stop complaining to themselves
about their wearisome journeys with Jesus. The next day,
their cross seemed remarkably lighter!

8

The Faith That Lives

James 1:19—2:26

> *Wherefore lay apart all filthiness and superfluity of naughtiness, and receive with meekness the engrafted word, which is able to save your souls. But be ye doers of the word, and not hearers only, deceiving your own selves* (Ja 1:21-22). *For as the body without the spirit is dead, so faith without works is dead also* (Ja 2:26).

Eventually, the Saviour's instructions about the way of the cross became fully fruitful in the lives of His disciples. Having learned for themselves what it meant to "save their lives" through selfless submission to their Master, they proclaimed this principle wherever they taught the Word of God. In particular, in Jerusalem, after the Lord Jesus had returned to the heavenly glory from which He had come, the disciples assisted in the formation of a Christian community for which this truth was of transcendent importance.

Indeed, in that infant fellowship of believers, self-sacrifice in the name of Jesus was a way of life (Ac 2:44-45). And it was there that James was nurtured in the early days of his faith, listening with all eagerness and hunger of heart to the teaching of the original followers of his Lord. He could not hear soon enough, nor be told often enough, all that his brother had laid down on this surpassing theme, and the concept of "saving one's life" soon passed into the very fiber of his being. Though he had not personally heard the Saviour's public pronouncements of this truth, by the time James became a teacher in the church it was a part of the warp and woof of his own ministry.

There had been, of course, certain occasions when he *had* heard his brother preach. And even then, in his unbelief, he had not failed to be impressed. Take Jesus' sermon on the mountain, for example. That had been delivered in Galilee early in the Saviour's ministry, and James happened to have been there. He never really forgot much of what his brother had said that day. Though he had not yet accepted from Jesus the "good and perfect" gift of life, his memory was marked by some of the striking phrases and unforgettable images that Jesus had employed.

Years later, after he had come to believe in his brother and had willingly become His "bond-servant," James recalled a large number of those memorable utterances and put them to use. If he spoke to his fellow Christians of the joy that could be theirs in the time of trial, it was not without remembering that Jesus had said, "Blessed are you, when men shall revile you, and persecute you, and say all manner of evil against you falsely, for My sake. Rejoice and be exceedingly glad, for great is your reward in heaven; for so they persecuted the prophets which were before you" (Mt 5:11-12). And if he spoke of the Father as One who gave every good and perfect gift, there was yet another recollection from that sermon lodged deep in his heart. "If you, being evil, know how to give good gifts to your children," Jesus had affirmed, "how much more shall your Father which is in heaven give good things to those who ask Him?" (Mt 7:11).

There were many other memories that James had from that mountain-top message, but few that more completely shaped his thinking than Jesus' final words that day. As long as he lived, he could recall them clearly. "Therefore," said Jesus, "whoever hears these words of mine, and does them, I will compare him to a wise man, who built his house upon a rock.

And the rain descended, and the floods came, and the winds blew, and beat upon that house, and it did not fall because it was founded upon a rock. And everyone who hears these words of mine and does not do them, shall be compared to a foolish man, who built his house upon the sand. And the rain descended, and the floods came, and the winds blew, and beat upon that house, and it fell; and great was its fall!" (Mt 7: 24-27).

And with that, Jesus had stopped speaking. It was an impressive conclusion, and the huge audience that had heard Him buzzed with comment. James remembered some of that comment and above all the frequently repeated observation that Jesus taught differently than the Jewish scribes (Mt 7: 28-29). For whereas those men were constantly appealing to the decisions and interpretations of Israel's greatest rabbis, Jesus appealed to no authority beyond Himself. He spoke as an oracle of God, and He asserted unequivocally the demands that His words placed on all who heard them. That was what the conclusion of His message had been all about. A man who heard *and did* His words was like a prudent builder whose house was secure from storm, but the man who heard and did them not was, by contrast, a foolish man whose building was destined for ruin.

James could recall, in later years, that he had thought at the time how logical the demand of Jesus actually was. It was not as a mere scribe of the Jewish law that his brother was presenting Himself to men, but instead as the Christ of God. Perhaps He did not usually make that claim explicit, but it was plainly implicit in all He said and did. Already there were many who claimed to have found eternal life through Him, and were boldly confessing Him as their Saviour. And it was evident that Jesus welcomed such faith, and encouraged it. It followed, therefore, James had realized, that if that was who his brother really was—though he could not for a moment believe it—then His words *did* carry all the weight He claimed for them.

In that case, the words of Jesus were the words of God with all of the supreme and holy authority which that fact implied.

Consequently, it was obvious that the figure of the two builders made superlatively good sense if one granted the premise that Jesus spoke the Word of God. The "house" which each of them built must signify their life, for a man "lives" in his house. It followed, therefore, that if Jesus' words were indeed the timeless truth of God, there was no other secure foundation on which a man could build his life.

Hearing those words, in that case, was not enough. One must by all means *do* them. For, the parable asserted emphatically, whenever a man's life was smitten by the storms and misfortunes which inevitably come to human experience, that life could only withstand the tests if it was firmly grounded on *doing* what Jesus said.

Obedience, therefore, was the key to endurance. A mere hearing, where Jesus' words were concerned, was dangerous. It was like building a house on sand without any consideration of what might happen in one good storm. As soon as the storm struck that house, it would collapse, leaving the life of the man who built it an irreparable shambles. Indeed, that life might even be terminated altogether, if the storm which struck it was the ultimate one of death itself. This much had been clear to James even then.

James could remember thinking at the time also that if he ever *did* believe in his brother, he would most certainly also become His disciple. In fact, at the very start of that unforgettable sermon, Jesus had deliberately and conspicuously singled His disciples out of the crowd, allowing them to come to Him and sit around Him while He spoke (Mt 5:1-2). Clearly He intended His audience to perceive that it was through discipleship to Himself that His utterances could be realized in their lives.

This, of course, implied that they must have faith in Him, but it implied more as well. It implied a willingness on their part to yield their lives to the redirection He would give them. In short, the house they lived in was to be built upon the foundation of His Word and in obedience to His specifications. Only thus could they be secure in storm. Later James was to realize that faith in Jesus brought to men the gift of life. Discipleship introduced them to doing God's will and work. By the former, they were begotten of God. By the latter, their lives were built up and preserved from ruin and loss.

Much time had now passed. James had become a leading figure in the Christian church at Jerusalem, with pastoral concerns that stretched far beyond that city. These were difficult days for the followers of Jesus, and persecution and testing of all kinds and descriptions seemed to afflict them frequently. And because these believers in God's Son were often materially poor, they were particularly exposed to the oppression of rich men who happened to reject the Saviour. More than once, some defenseless Christian had been hauled into court on trumped up charges by some blasphemous man of wealth. Such experiences were like violent storms sweeping down on their lives, and they desperately needed the advice and counsel of a spiritual shepherd.

Such a shepherd James had now become. Believing in Jesus, his brother after the flesh but also the Lord of glory, he now served Him as a "bond-servant." The Saviour's interests were now James' interests, the Saviour's concerns his concerns as well. In writing to a widely scattered collection of Christian churches, therefore, James sought to give advice to his troubled readers like the advice he felt his Lord would give had He been here to do it. Thus the words that he inscribed on the papyrus sheet before him were saturated with principles drawn from the teachings of Jesus, especially those He had laid down in His sermon on the mountain.

Following the salutation of his letter, James came right to the point. Were his readers burdened by "many-colored" testings? Let them rejoice in them. The Saviour would have told them to! Were they in need of wisdom in their time of trial? Let them ask for it from God, the Father whom Jesus said knew how to give good gifts to those who asked Him. But if, in their troubles, they felt tempted to do evil, let them be careful not to blame such feelings on a generous God. From the urge to sin, only death could come. From the Father of lights, only good and perfect gifts (Ja 1:1-18).

"Let no man say when he is tempted that 'I am being tempted by God,' because," wrote James, "God cannot be tempted by evil nor does He Himself tempt any man. But every man is tempted when he is drawn away and enticed by his own lusts. Then lust after it has become pregnant gives birth to sin, and sin when it has matured, gives birth to death. Do not go astray, my beloved brothers. Every good gift and every perfect gift is from above, coming down from the Father of lights with whom there is no variation, nor shadow cast by turning. Of His own will He begot us with the word of truth."

Never blame God for your temptations to sin, James was saying. To do so is to misunderstand the very character of God, who cannot be tempted with evil, and to misjudge His activity. God never tempts a man to sin. A man's own inward lust does that. Rather, God gives good and perfect gifts. Moreover, lust is like a wicked woman of the streets which, through forming an affinity with our hearts, becomes pregnant with a sinful act. When that act is born—in short, when we do what lust prompts us to do—that act becomes the daughter of our wrong desire, capable of growing in its consequences until maturity is attained and a new child is born. And that child is death! But that is the offspring of our lust, through sin, and not in any way the offspring of the Father of lights! We, however, *are* His offspring, for "of His own will He begat us with the word of truth"!

And there it stood in language as plain as James could make it. We have indeed received the good and perfect gift of life eternal, and by its means we have become God's children.

But that fact, wonderful though it is, does not annul the capacity of the heart to sin. Our divine birth is by the word of truth, a living seed implanted in our being. But the fruit of that seed depends altogether on what is allowed to go on in the heart into which it now has entered.

Jesus had taught that if rocky soil was in the heart, the seed could attain no depth. If thorns were there, it could attain no maturity. And, says James, if *lust* is there, the individual who fulfills that lust may *die!* Never confuse the two, James insisted. By the Father's gift, we have eternal life. As the consequence of sin, we may experience physical death.

The principle James was enunciating was as old as the ancient scriptures on which he had been reared in that godly home at Nazareth. Long ago Solomon, the wisest of men, had observed, "The fear of the Lord prolongs days, but the years of the wicked shall be shortened" (Pr 10:27) and "As righteousness tends to life, so he that pursues evil, pursues it to his own death" (Pr 11:19). And also, "The law of the wise is a fountain of life, to depart from the snares of death" (Pr 13:14). There was no question about it. The prolongation of one's days on earth was facilitated by a righteous life. Their premature termination was the all too frequent consequence of sin. James' statement, therefore, was undeniably true. "Sin, when it has matured, gives birth to death!"

Having contrasted thus God's gift of life with sin's "gift" of death, James is now ready in his letter to drive home a practical piece of advice. He wants his Christian readers, begotten as they are by the word of truth, to avoid the death-dealing consequences of any unrighteous behavior that they were tempted to indulge in under the pressure of their troubles. He wants, in short, to save their lives. The avoidance of sin alone could, in a real sense, accomplish this end. But James also realized that the concept of saving the life had received a new dimension in the teaching of Jesus.

By means of paradox, which the Saviour was so fond of

using, Jesus had taught that a man's life could be saved even when it was lost! Of course He demanded righteousness to achieve this end, just as the Old Testament demanded it for the prolonging of one's days. But the righteousness Jesus insisted on was worked out in discipleship, by which men were called to take up their cross and follow Him. And even if that path led to a martyr's death, still the life was saved.

Indeed, in a real sense the life might be lost *day by day* as one sacrificed personal interests to do the will of God, but in the process his eternal preservation was being worked out. For such a life could never really end—even when, paradoxically, it did—because its value and worth would last forever.

Thus, the Old Testament concept of extending one's life had been superbly transformed in the teaching of Jesus. According to the Old Testament doctrine, righteousness extended one's life and postponed the grave. According to Jesus' doctrine, discipleship extended one's life *beyond* the grave. In both cases, the life was saved, but the richer and deeper sense belonged to the precepts of Jesus. As James prepares to write his practical counsel, he has both concepts in mind.

"Of His own will He begat us with the word of truth, that we should be a kind of firstfruits of His creatures," James had just written. Now he proceeds, "Therefore, my beloved brothers, let every man be quick to hear, slow to speak, slow to anger. For man's anger does not accomplish God's righteousness. Therefore, lay aside all filthiness and the superfluity of wickedness, and receive with meekness the implanted word, *which is able to save your souls.*"

How practical James' words were for his readers in the midst of their testings. Under the pressure of trial and difficulty, they were sometimes tempted to blame God for an insidious inward desire to do evil. After all, He allowed them to have trouble. Yet, the desire to sin came from the lust in their hearts, while the God they felt like blaming was the very one whose good and perfect gift of life they had so freely received. By the word of truth He had actually begotten them.

What then should they do? Blame so generous a God for their own sin? Perish the thought! Now, if ever, was the time to listen to the Word of God. It was, therefore, a time for hearing, not for speaking, and certainly not for impatient anger. God's righteousness would never be worked out in their lives by anger! No, they must lay aside their tendencies to evil, and humbly receive instruction from the very word by which they had been born anew. That word of truth had already made them a sort of firstfruits of God's creatures. Now it could save their souls!

"Save your souls!" For one who read these words in Greek, the language in which James was now writing, the words meant equally well, "Save your *lives.*" Indeed, the expression was verbally the same as Jesus' own when He said, "Whoever wants to save his life . . ." Thus, in the Greek tongue, the word "soul" and "life" were one. There were, of course, other words for life, but this one in particular suggested the intrinsic, inner self which was *alive* and capable of experiencing all that human existence could offer. It was "life," therefore, conceived of as inseparable from selfhood.

"Save your lives"? What did James mean? Clearly, at the very least, the deadly consequences of sin would be averted if they gave true heed to God's Word. Physical life, therefore, could be extended by humble submission to God's truth, as one laid aside his own filthiness and rejected wickedness as a worthless superfluity of his experience. But saving the life was more than that, as Jesus Himself had taught. It was the capacity of a man's life to withstand every storm, every test, every trouble—even death itself—so that the basic structure and value of that life endured beyond the grave.

And it was just here that James' mind inevitably worked its way back to the parable of the two builders which he had heard in that sermon on the mountain so many years ago. From that parable it was clear that the life lived in discipleship to Jesus had a resilience in time of trouble that was totally lacking in a life that was not so lived. The disciple was nothing less than a prudent builder who founded his life—his house—on solid bedrock. And that rock, Jesus had made clear, was His *Word!*

The parable of Jesus did not merely teach that the house upon the rock lasted *longer* than the house upon the sand. Rather, it taught that the former *lasted,* while the other did not. Thus it unmistakably hinted that a man whose life is built on the words of the Saviour is a man whose life nothing— not even death—can destroy, while a man whose life is not so built is a man whose life many things—but *especially* death— can overturn in ruins. The word of Jesus, therefore, was the secret of saving one's life in the ultimate sense of that truth.

"Receive with meekness the implanted word which is able to save your lives." How James' readers needed to hear that! Buffeted as they were by troubles, tempted often to sin, they needed to know where to find real bedrock for their lives. They needed to learn how to give to their lives a security and solidity which none of the vicissitudes of their stormy experience could touch. The word of truth is your secret, says James. The implanted word can preserve your lives—be it for time or eternity.

The *implanted* word! The term evoked an image from nature, but in general use it signified "innate." The word that saves the life is "innate" to you, James was saying. You are no strangers to that word, for through it you were begotten by the Father of lights. Hence it is an "inborn" word because by it you were "born in" to the family of God. Like a seed planted in the soil of your heart, God's Word is now native to your being. It is, therefore, something which it is most natural for you to respond to.

Yet be sure you do respond, James continued to write. "But be doers of the word, and not hearers only, deceiving your own selves. For if anyone is a hearer of the word, and not a doer, he is like a man gazing at the face he was born with, in a mirror. For he gazes and goes away, and at once he forgets what sort of person he was. But whoever peers into the perfect law of liberty, and perseveres—this man not being a forgetful hearer but a doer of work—the same man shall be blessed in his doing."

The parable of Jesus was now ringing in James' ears. "Whoever hears these words of mine and does them, I will compare him to a wise man." And, "Everyone who hears these words of mine and does not do them, shall be compared to a foolish man." The one who hears and does versus the one who only hears had been the contrast presented by the Saviour, and it was now the contrast set forth by James. How foolish it was to be merely a hearer of the Word and not a doer of it also! So foolish, in fact, that it was comparable to a man who studied himself in a mirror and then immediately forgot what it was he looked like. Obviously a piece of sheer stupidity!

But there was more to James' new imagery than that. In an ordinary mirror a man might see the face he had by natural birth, "the face he was born with." But in the word of truth a man might see the face he had by his birth from above. There he might discern "what sort of person he was," now that he was born of God. Indeed the Word of God into which he was to look was an "innate" word, native to his inner being, because with it he had been begotten by the Father of lights. It was an excellent mirror, therefore, in which to see what the grace of God had made him.

In the natural world of men, a single glance into a mirror might suffice to hopelessly enamor a man with the appearance of his natural face. It was, in any case, an appearance he was not likely to soon forget. Why then, in spiritual matters, should a man not be enamored by the wondrous visage that was his as a child of God?

"Of His own will He begat us . . . that we might be a sort of firstfruits of His creatures." A firstfruits of His creatures? What a vision to catch sight of in the divine looking glass! To discern indeed that by our birth from above we are men possessing the capacity to reflect the purity and holiness of the world to come! To discover that, after all, we are God's workmanship created for the good works He has prepared for us to walk in! What a radiant spiritual countenance to behold in the mirror of God's Word! The very likeness of Jesus is there, and that's what manner of men we are because the Saviour's life is in us. How could we behold and then forget? Yet that was precisely what we did every time we heard and did not do His word. It was the height of folly.

But conversely, James was saying, if we are wise enough to peer attentively into the mirror of God's Word, and persevere in that Word by doing it and not just hearing it only, *then* true blessing will be ours. After all, the Word into which we are to look with obedient hearts is not a law of bondage but a law of freedom. Had not Jesus once said to some who believed in Him, "If you continue in My word, then you are My disciples really; and you shall know the truth, and the truth shall set you free"? Yes, these had been His words, to which He had then added, "Whoever commits sin is the bond-slave of sin" (Jn 8: 31-32, 36). So it was sin which robbed men of their truest freedom. But it was discipleship to Jesus, persisting obediently in His Word, that gave it back.

Such then was the only true course of wisdom. As those who have been born from above, James was saying, you must each set it as your unflinching purpose to be, not a forgetful hearer, but a *doer* of God's Word.

And so it happened that, in the letter he was writing, James was teaching the same truth that Jesus Himself had taught in His sermon on the mountain. In the midst of the troubles and storms of human experience, the life of a man—his house—was saved by God's Word *if* he heard *and did it*. Thus it had an eternal worth that not even death could shake. But if he was a hearer only, he was risking a colossal disaster. He was consigning his earthly experience to tragic ruins.

There it was again! The water and the food! The gift of God on the one hand, freely bestowed and eternally unfailing. And on the other hand, the call of discipleship to do the will of God and to finish His work! Jesus had spoken of both things at the well of Sychar. And in the hands of James these twin truths found fresh and vital exposition. Birth from above was utterly without human effort. "Of His own will, He begot us," James said. But the preservation of one's life required works.

"But whoever peers into the perfect law of liberty, and perseveres—this man not being a forgetful hearer but a doer of work—the same man shall be blest in his doing." If the blessing of God, therefore, was to rest truly and fully on the life of any whom He had begotten, that person must by all means be a worker. Only thus could the life be saved.

Presently, as his letter continued, James went on to spell out some of the works which the Christian conscience commended. One such work was realized by practical, down-to-earth generosity to those in need—particularly the fatherless and the widows. Another good work involved an even-handed, impartial treatment of rich and poor alike in the local Christian church, so that the rich man was not favored nor the poor man despised. In short, mercy in all its forms and expressions was to be assiduously cultivated, for the merciful man was ever the recipient of the mercy of God.

And mercy was what man needed most in his hour of trouble and storm. If the judgment of God fell, unrelieved by any mercy, upon the house a man had built—upon his life—how could it survive? What could save him from the disaster and ruin which *that* would bring? Could mere faith, unaccompanied by works, save him? Some of James' readers evidently thought so. Simply because they were believers in the one true God, and in His Son the Lord Jesus Christ, they expected God to vindicate them in their troubles, to justify them before men in their time of testing. When the storms came, they expected God's mercy and deliverance from trouble to be theirs automatically because they were people of faith.

That was a great mistake, James went on to point out. In the hour of testing, a man needs more than faith to come through successfully. He needs *works!* Think of the patriarch Abraham. How did he pass *his* supreme test, when he was called upon to sacrifice his very own son? How was *he* vindicated in *his* trial so that he earned the title "friend of God"? By faith alone? No! But by a faith that *worked,* producing obedience to the Word of God which had come to him!

And consider Rahab, whose story James' readers knew from the book of Joshua. How did she pass *her* test, when Jericho, her city, was about to be reduced to ruins and all its people killed? Was *her life* saved by faith alone? Once again, no! Rather by her works—the help she actually furnished the messengers who came to her—she survived. And thus she too was justified, vindicated in an hour of potential calamity by works.

Do you wish to be vindicated in your troubles as truly righteous people? James was asking. If so, you will be justified by works. Faith alone is not enough for *this kind* of justification. For the only kind of faith which can save a life is the kind of faith which is itself *alive* and *working!* "For as the body without the spirit is dead, so faith without works is dead also."

James' readers were not dead! At least, not yet! But "sin, when it has matured, gives birth to death." That was a solemn thought. And obedience to God's implanted word was the only preventative for that. Not mere affirmation that that word was true. Not mere hearing. But *doing!* The kind of faith, therefore, which responded obediently to the truth of God, that kind of faith—and that alone—was truly vital and alive. Faith was like a body which required the animation of an inward spirit. Without, therefore, the quickening influence of good works in one's life, faith died and became a mere corpse in a man's experience. Real enough it might be, tangible like a lifeless body was tangible, but equally inactive and dormant. And a dead faith could certainly not save one's life!

Years before James wrote these words, the Lord Jesus had spoken of the seed which fell on stony ground. Little shoots had sprung up at once, then died. In interpreting His own figure, the Saviour had explained how those transient shoots exposed a temporary faith in the individuals He described. "Who believe for a while, but *in time of testing,* turn away." Their troubles as believers in Him had been too much for them, and their faith had withered away and died. Pretty soon it was gone altogether, blown away, as it were, by the violent winds of adversity, for "in time of testing, they turn away." Of course, the life of God within them had not vanished, for the spring of living water continued to gush up into eternal life, just as Jesus had promised. But the vital seed of that life was now fruitless, hidden from view in some crack or crevice of its rocky home.

And such was a real and present danger to every believer in the Saviour who confronted the storms of life. Unless he saw to it that the vitality of his faith was maintained by the constant reanimation of a life of good works—a life securely built on obedience to God—that faith could wither and die. And if it died, it might disappear altogether, decomposing so to speak like a corpse, and buried for good beneath a barren and wasted experience.

So, James insisted, keep your faith alive by working at it. Build your house securely on the will and Word of God.

9

The Riches of the World to Come

James 2:5

> *And seeing the multitudes, he went up into a mountain: and when he was set, his disciples came unto him: And he opened his mouth, and taught them, saying, Blessed are the poor in spirit: for their's is the kingdom of heaven* (Mt 5: 1-3).

> *And he lifted up his eyes on his disciples, and said, Blessed be ye poor, for your's is the kingdom of God* (Lk 6:20). *Hearken, my beloved brethren, Hath not God chosen the poor of this world rich in faith, and heirs of the kingdom which he hath promised to them that love him?* (Ja 2:5).

Both Jesus and James had grown up in a home that was poor. A little less than six weeks after Jesus was born, Joseph and Mary had presented Him before God in the temple at Jerusalem in accordance with the Jewish law. But they had been unable to afford the lamb which was prescribed as a sacrifice on that occasion, so they had taken advantage of Moses' provision for the poor. They had offered a pigeon instead (Lev 12:6-8; Lk 2:21-24). Joseph himself was a humble carpenter, and it was not easy for him to provide for the large family of boys and girls which he and Mary were raising. Jesus and James, therefore, had learned from childhood how to be satisfied with little more than the basic necessities of life. Yet, though there was poverty in their home, there was dignity as well; and they had never felt ashamed.

In later years, after he had come to believe in Jesus, James had often pondered the astounding reality that the Son of God had left the undimmed splendor of heaven to live in a home like that. How well He might have chosen some richer dwelling—a royal palace, had He so desired—but instead He had chosen James' home with all its material lacks and needs, and there He had been content to grow up. What a comment that was, James could not help but think, upon the low esteem in which God held the wealth of earth. How clearly it suggested that whatever might be truly riches in the eyes of the heavenly Father, they were not the riches of this age.

And whenever he thought that way, he always remembered once more that unforgettable sermon on the mountain. How full his mind was of recollections from that message! Little had he dreamed at the time, that the brother in whom he could not then believe was nevertheless powerfully shaping his convictions by the words He uttered on that occasion. Only now did James perceive what vital and transforming words they had proved to be. And among those words James could not forget, were these: "Lay not up for yourselves treasures upon earth, where moth and rust corrupt, and where thieves break through and steal. But lay up for yourselves treasures in heaven, where neither moth nor rust corrupt, and where thieves do not break through nor steal. For where your treasure is, there will your heart be also" (Mt 6:19-21). As much or more than any other words he ever heard, these had molded James' concept of genuine wealth. The true riches were not those which men store up here, but those which they store up for the hereafter.

"For where your treasure is there will your heart be also." *How true,* James had thought even then. A man lived for what was truly valuable to him. If, therefore, the things he valued most were those he could store up in this life, he lived for them. But if his most treasured hopes were such as could be realized only in the age to come, he would fix his heart on that unseen world and live for it. But it took *faith* to reject the former kind of riches and to prefer the latter. For the riches of earth were visible, tangible, and accessible in the here and now, while those of heaven were presently unseen and unexperienced. From the very first, therefore, James had sensed that to become a man of wealth in the kingdom of God required much faith, for it required the capacity to grasp the realities of a future world and to set one's heart on them unswervingly.

This, of course, was much more than the faith by which men appropriated God's gift of life eternal. For that, a single moment of simple, childlike trust was all that God required. It took but a single drink of the Saviour's living water to fix forever the destiny of the drinker, who could never thirst again. But far more than a moment of faith was required if one were determined to lay up treasures in heaven, while rejecting the allurements of the treasures of earth. To make a choice like that, and to maintain that choice to the end of life, clearly required a faith that was both robust and very abundant. Thus, as James came eventually to perceive, the wealth of that future age would surely belong to those who possessed a wealth of faith right here and now.

But what of those, like some Christians James knew, who had little more than the faith they started with when first they believed in the Saviour? Suppose through lack of a rich and luxuriant faith they continued to live largely for the satisfactions of this life, rather than for those of the life to come? Did it not follow, with irresistible logic, that if wealth in God's kingdom depended on fulfilling the Saviour's command to lay it up, then one who ignored that command would find himself— by comparison—poor in that day? *Surely it followed,* James thought.

In fact, as James now saw most clearly, in a sense there would be rich and poor in that future age just as there were rich and poor in this present one. All who entered that splendid world would do so by virtue of receiving the gift of God in simple faith. But all who acquired the treasures of that world would do so by virtue of their wealth of faith through which they laid those treasures up. No wonder, therefore, that Jesus had chosen a home of poverty while here on earth! For here it mattered not if one were poor. That could only matter in the day to come.

Moreover, James now knew as well, the distinction between "rich" and "poor" in the kingdom of God described precisely the difference in destiny between the disciple and the nondisciple. The disciple was one who, with vitality of faith in Jesus, denied himself, took up his cross daily, and devotedly followed the Saviour. It was he who saved his life while seeming, paradoxically, to lose it. But the nondisciple was one who, through meagerness of faith, pursued a path of worldly self-indulgence only to hopelessly lose the life he had so desperately sought to preserve. For the former, measureless eternal wealth awaited him at the end of life's road; for the latter, sad loss and embarrassing poverty.

Both would most certainly enter God's kingdom—that was God's gift—but the one would have so much more to enjoy there than the other that no other terms could adequately appraise the qualitative distinction between them than the words "wealth" and "poverty."

James no longer looked at rich men with that twinge of envy he had sometimes felt when still a boy. How fleeting and transient was the wealth such men possessed! How quickly it was gone—and life itself—impoverishing its proud possessor so that he left the world exactly as he entered it, empty-handed. Who could envy an experience like that? Or even desire it? Was it not so much better to follow the Saviour, to experience whatever deprivation that course might entail, and thus to become rich toward God? What did it matter to have riches here, but poverty hereafter? Better by far to be poor now if one could be rich then.

In fact, James realized, there was a sense in which it was

essential to be poor now in order to be rich then. And once again, the Master's words in His sermon on the mountain had been formative in James' perceptions. Indeed, he remembered clearly the crucial utterance with which that sermon opened: "Blessed are the poor in spirit, for theirs is the kingdom of heaven." And he remembered too that this utterance had been pointedly directed by Jesus at His disciples, who had just come out of the crowds to sit before Him. It seemed evident, therefore, that Jesus had meant to indicate that poverty of spirit was to be a leading feature of His true disciples and that ownership of God's kingdom was its fitting reward.

Later James had understood this more clearly. A genuine disciple was one who emptied his human spirit of pride and self-will and who meekly submitted his life to the authority of Jesus, following Him wherever He led. Divesting himself of the stubborn self-interest to which men cling as they might cling to a priceless treasure, the disciple was to become truly "poor in spirit." To such people, Jesus declared, the kingdom of heaven belonged.

James had learned much from the sermon on the mountain. He had not, however, had the privilege of hearing the sermon on the plain. The original disciples, however, had heard it, and from them James was not surprised to learn that the Saviour had begun that discourse in a manner very much the same. For then, too, the Lord Jesus had commenced His message by fixing His gaze pointedly on the disciples themselves and saying, "Blessed are you, the poor, for yours is the kingdom of God." That, James at first had thought, corresponded exactly to the words he had heard earlier on the mountainside. Yet, upon later reflection, he realized that there was also a difference. On the mountain Jesus had said, "Blessed are the poor *in spirit,*" but on the plain He had simply stated, "Blessed are you, *the poor!*"

This distinction deserved some thought, James had realized. What was the relationship between poverty and poverty of spirit? It was evident that no one could truly possess the kingdom of God unless he were in some sense poor, but did that mean that literal poverty somehow furnished a better environment in which to cultivate spiritual poverty as well?

Then he thought of Jesus and their home in Nazareth. How superlative an example of spiritual meekness and submission to God his own brother had supplied, coming down from resplendent heavenly glory to live in a home like that and then to die for the sins of men. In Jesus, surely, material poverty and sublime poverty of spirit had been perfectly combined. Indeed, no one appreciated better than James the supernal truth that Paul was later to express, "For you know the grace of our Lord Jesus Christ, that, though He was rich, yet for your sakes He became poor, that you through His poverty might be rich" (2 Co 8:9). And thus impressed, James could not help but believe that the example of the Master had a voice for all His followers. True submission to God, true dedication to the wealth of the age to come, was like a rare and exquisite flower. It flourished best in the fertile soil of earthly poverty.

Not of course that the rich could never become "poor in spirit." But they found the becoming so extremely hard. To begin with it was hard enough for a rich man even to *enter* the kingdom of God, much less to qualify to *possess* it. In fact, James had often heard the disciples tell of a sadly disappointing interview the Saviour had had one day with a wealthy young inquirer. And on that occasion Jesus had affirmed emphatically, "How hardly shall they that have riches enter into the kingdom of God!" Of course at the time the disciples had been shocked by this. Like most of their fellow countrymen, they supposed that if a man was rich God's blessing must truly rest upon him.

But Jesus answered their amazement with a further statement which they never forgot. "Children," He had said most gently, "how hard it is for those who *trust in riches* to enter into the kingdom of God! It is easier for a camel to go through the eye of a needle than for a rich man to enter into the kingdom of God" (Mk 10:23-27). Naturally that explained it. To gain entrance into the heavenly kingdom, God insisted that men should trust, with childlike simplicity, in the gift He could give them through His Son. But the rich man tended to trust his riches. Whatever he needed he could buy, and it was hard for him to accept so priceless a gift and pay nothing in return. Like an overloaded camel, vainly seeking to slip through the tiniest of holes, the rich man was too "big," too confident in the wealth with which he was laden, to pass easily through so restricted, yet so simple, an entrance way into life eternal.

Yet it could happen, of course, and Jesus had assured His disciples of that. "With men it is impossible," He had said, "but not with God, for with God all things are possible." And just as no man could ever push a camel through a needle's eye, no more could human persuasion bring a self-confident rich man to trust in Christ, and Christ alone. But God could do it. And James now knew quite well that everywhere the gospel had been preached there were men of wealth—not many, but a few—whose eyes God had opened to receive the gift of life.

But obviously, if it was so hard for the well-to-do to gain entrance into the kingdom of God by so simple an act of faith, it was immeasurably harder for them by a whole life of faith to gain *possession* of that kingdom. Time and time again experience had shown how rarely the soil in a rich man's heart was truly fertile ground for the life-bestowing seed of the Saviour's Word. Usually that soil was filled with thorns—the jagged, tearing goads of care and wealth and worldly pleasure. Only seldom did the gospel seed bear full and abundant fruitage in the life of a man of wealth. It could happen—with God all things were possible—but it did not happen often.

Thus an impressive paradox emerged. James could not escape its truth. Clearly, in the very nature of the case, the roles of poverty and wealth tended to be reversed when this age was compared with the age to come. In this world, the rich rarely accepted the gift of God, but when they did their faith tended to remain shriveled and weak. Conversely, the poor, when *they* received that gift, had little on earth in which they could put their trust, except in the Saviour who had given them life.

Hence, the rich tended to be poor in faith and the poor man tended to be rich in faith. And while the rich man was often hindered from a true discipleship by his preoccupation with the treasures of earth, the poor man could devote his whole life to storing away the treasures of heaven. No wonder, therefore, that Jesus had told His followers on one occasion, "Fear not, little flock, because it is your Father's good pleasure *to give you* the kingdom. Sell what belongs to you and give to charity. Make for yourselves purses which do not get old, a treasure in the heavens that does not fail, where the thief does not draw near nor does the moth corrupt. For where your treasure is, there will your heart be also" (Lk 12:32-34).

How much better it would be, James felt, to divest oneself completely of earthly goods, than to allow those goods to deprive one of so glorious a future possession. It was the Father's good pleasure to *give* the kingdom to those who sacrificially followed His Son. *That,* it was plain, was the priceless treasure men were to invest in for the age to come. And if for any given individual the faith required for this grew better in soil less richly endowed with earthly treasure, that was the soil in which such faith should be most carefully nurtured by him. If to become poor in spirit one needed to become poor, then clearly it was well worth doing. For the utterance of Jesus remained timelessly valid. "Blessed are you, the poor"—at least in spirit, at most completely poor—"for yours is the kingdom of God."

Now James was a leader in the Christian church at Jerusalem. In the pastoral letter which he found it necessary to write to his beloved but frequently troubled Christian brothers, he had warned them sternly against playing favorites with the rich men who might come to their church (Ja 2:1-4). It was a real temptation, especially since the patronage of a rich man might stand them in good stead in a moment of crisis. But in the process it was easy to slight some poor man, to steer him to some inferior seat, and to treat him as though he amounted to very little or nothing at all.

That, however, might prove to be a disastrous misjudgment, James was careful to point out. Despite the fact that the rich man they honored might be dressed in the most elegant of garments and be sporting on his finger a brilliant golden ring, while the poor man they slighted might be dirty and disheveled, the poor man might actually be the richer of the two! "Listen, my beloved brothers," James penned with emphasis, "has not God chosen the poor of this world to be rich in faith, and heirs of the kingdom which He has promised to those that love Him?" (Ja 2:5).

Yes, it was true and it was precisely what James had learned from the humble life and pointed teachings of the brother who was now his Lord. Rich men there might be who had heard and believed the gospel of God's Son, and one might expect them to appear from time to time at the meetings of a Christian church. But too often their faith was miserably small. Though they had accepted the gift of eternal life, beyond that they found it hard to trust God in any deep and consistent way.

Conversely, the poor man who came to faith in Christ seemed somehow to learn very quickly the many lessons of faith which trouble and deprivation could teach him. The rich man could fall back, he thought, on his prestige and resources in time of testing, but the poor man had little to fall back on but God. Thus that priceless commodity of confidence in God which James' readers urgently needed in their variegated experiences of testing, was the very thing the poor man was very likely to have abundantly acquired, while the rich man remained stunted, a spiritual pauper in the midst of his material plenty.

In fact, it often seemed that the quantity of a man's faith was in inverse proportion to the quantity of his wealth. It was a serious mistake, therefore, for James' readers to pass a superficial judgment on the basis of what a man wore. It was the poor man, despite his rags, who often was truly rich, "rich in faith."

But those who were "rich in faith" were also "heirs of the kingdom" which God had promised "to those that love Him." *Heirs* of the kingdom. That was something more than merely getting into it. That was to have a prospect of great wealth in that kingdom.

A person might enter the mansion of a rich man, he might survey all its splendid furnishings and appointments, he might even live in it if permitted to do so, but he would own nothing that was there. Unless he had a valid claim in accordance with the established laws of ownership or inheritance, he might personally be a man of poverty even while he dwelt surrounded by priceless abundance. The mansion was where he lived, but it was not truly his.

And so it would be in the kingdom of God. Entrance into that kingdom was assured to all whom the Father of lights had freely begotten with His word of truth. But to inherit that kingdom—to truly possess it, with all its honors and privileges, as one's own—one must become, right now, "rich in faith."

"Except a man be born again, he cannot see the kingdom of God" (Jn 3:3). Such were the words of Jesus, and since birth from above was a gift from the Father of lights, one could expect to see that kingdom and could expect to enter it, on the grounds of God's gracious generosity alone. But *seeing* a thing and *owning* it were two different propositions. And while mere access to God's kingdom was an unspeakable privilege, fraught with wondrous eternal joys, there was incomparably more to be had than that. Indeed how splendid it must be to *possess* the kingdom could only be guessed from the fact that those who merely entered it could be thought of as "poor." Blessed poverty, no doubt!

But conversely, its opposite must be unimaginable wealth.

Indeed, James' own mind was often staggered by that thought as he tried to penetrate the veil through which man can but dimly discern the glistening glories and unspeakable privileges of an eternal world. And even the merest glimpse of them sufficed to cast a pall of sordid cheapness over all that this age described as treasure.

How wondrous then must be the ultimate worth of the Saviour's words, "for *yours* is the kingdom of God"! How rich such an heirship must be! All of the measureless joys and blessings of heaven's coming reign upon the earth—all these, inherited by those who are poor in spirit and rich in faith. Could there ever be a more clarion call to true discipleship? Could there ever be a more compelling inducement to the pathway of self-denial and bearing the cross? James, at least, could not think of any.

For here was the shining goal that raised one's gratitude to a generous Saviour to the level of utter devotion. His gift of life alone was more than enough to inspire a lifetime of loyalty in all who had received it. But to share His kingdom and glory and to be able to call that kingdom "ours" as well? That was more than mortal man could dare imagine were it not the Son of God Himself who promised it. But promise it He had, and James could not help but love Him for it.

And that was exactly the point! "Heirs of the kingdom which He has promised *to those that love Him!*" Not to those who loved earthly wealth or earthly pleasure, but to those who loved *Him!* And again, the words of that mountain sermon were ringing in James' heart. "No man can serve two masters; for either he will hate the one and love the other, or else he will hold to the one and despise the other. You cannot serve God and wealth" (Mt 6:24). The choice must be made. No disciple could avoid it. Either the Lord Jesus would be loved, or the world would be loved, but one could not love them both. For those who had little in life to begin with it was easier to choose God and to grow rich in faith. For those who had much, this choice was harder and more rarely made.

Thus God had truly "chosen" the poor of this world to be rich in faith, for He had granted them precisely those circumstances in life in which such faith could grow and flourish. How thankful James was for the Nazareth home he had shared with the Saviour! What a blessing to be poor in the life that is now, if it led one to wealth in the life which was coming!

It was rather late in life, James felt, that he had come to perceive all this. Some of the original disciples of Jesus, men like Peter and John, had a long headstart along the pathway to eternal riches. But James had now fallen in step behind them. He wished that every Christian might do the same.

10

For the One Who Is Thirsty

Revelation 21:1-8; 22:16-17

> *And he that sat upon the throne said, Behold, I make all things new. And he said unto me, Write: for these words are true and faithful. And he said unto me, It is done. I am Alpha and Omega, the beginning and the end. I will give unto him that is athirst of the fountain of the water of life freely. He that overcometh shall inherit all things; and I will be his God, and he shall be my son. But the fearful, and unbelieving, and the abominable, and murderers, and whoremongers, and sorcerers, and idolaters, and all liars, shall have their part in the lake which burneth with fire and brimstone: which is the second death* (Rev 21:5-8).
>
> *And the Spirit and the bride say, Come. And let him that heareth say, come. And let him that is athirst come. And whosover will, let him take the water of life freely* (Rev 22:17).

Peter and John did have a long headstart on James. And while James had remained at home, not yet a believer in Jesus, Peter and John and the rest of the twelve disciples had followed the Master about as He sowed the quickening seed of the word of the gospel. And for all but Judas, who had never really received God's gift at all and whose discipleship was the merest pretense (Jn 6:64, 70-71), every step of the way made them just a little bit richer in the world to come.

But there were none of those twelve men who had traversed the pathway of a disciple longer than the apostle John. In fact, he was one of the two earliest of Jesus' followers; Andrew, Simon Peter's brother, being the other (Jn 1:35-40). Thus John had been among the disciples who had traveled with Jesus to Sychar, just as he had been among those who sat before Him as He preached the sermon on the mountain. Over the years of his companionship with his Lord, he had felt a growing closeness to his Master that was wonderful indeed.

When, therefore, that fateful night had come, and Jesus was eating His last supper with the disciples just before He died, it was John who had reclined right next to Him at the low table on which the Passover meal was spread. Propped up on his left elbow, with feet extending away from the table, John could easily lean his head back on the breast of Jesus who, in identical fashion, was reclining just behind him. And when, during the course of that meal, he had wanted to ask the Saviour a question, this is exactly what John did (Jn 13:23-25). His had been, therefore, a place of privileged nearness at that touching, memorable dinner.

Moreover, as James and the other brothers were to learn shortly after the crucifixion, John was the disciple to whom Jesus had committed the care of His mother (Jn 19:26-27). Not to His own brothers, still unbelieving, but to this devoted follower who had been with Him from the beginning. Clearly, John the son of Zebedee had as intimate a relationship to his Master as anyone else on earth.

Special tasks, therefore, had been reserved by the Saviour for this intimate follower of His. To begin with, he was later to write an account of Jesus' work on earth that was markedly distinct from the other accounts which the Spirit of God inspired.

For one thing, the gospel of John, unlike those of Matthew and Mark and Luke, stretches its narrative back into the earliest portions of Jesus' activity as a teacher. And among those early segments of His ministry which John alone records, there is the report of the conversations at Sychar's well. The crucial revelations unfolded there about the living water of eternal life and about the supernatural food of the obedient disciple are to be found only on the pages of John's book. Nor could the reader of God's Word afford to be without them, for the remaining three gospels are like giant storerooms, whose abundant supplies of truth are unlocked only by the key that John provides. In short, the later teachings of Jesus—as recorded by Matthew and Mark and Luke—are only genuinely comprehended if they are read in the light of what the Saviour had clearly taught from the beginning. And these foundational teachings of Jesus, it became John's prerogative to unfold.

But if John's perspective stretched back to the *earliest* revelations which were made by God's Son, at a later time he was to record His *final* revelations as well. For so it happened that John wrote also the last book of the Bible. Accordingly, it might be said that John was granted the privilege of reporting the Alpha and Omega—the A and the Z—the beginning and the end of God's truth as He unveiled it in Jesus Christ, our Lord.

A disciple John had been, therefore, from the very earliest period of the Saviour's ministry, and that discipleship had now spanned more than half a century. Though he was presently an old man, yet, even as he writes the Bible's final book, he knows what it means to take up his cross daily to follow Jesus. "I John," he writes in the opening chapter of that book, "who am your brother, and companion in the tribulation and kingdom and endurance of Jesus Christ, was in the island that is called Patmos, for the sake of the word of God and the testimony of Jesus Christ" (Rev 1:9). And so there he was, an exile, banished by Roman authority to a tiny spot of land in the Aegean Sea some thirty-five miles off the coast of Asia Minor. And for what crime? For nothing other than his fearless proclamation of the Word of God and for his ringing testimony to Jesus Christ.

But how could he have done anything else? For some fifty years and more, he had been eating the food of a disciple, the food he had once not known but now had grown to love. Into the harvest fields of God, therefore, he had been vigorously entering all this time, sowing the life-bearing seed of the word of truth, and reaping souls into God's barn. That had been the course of John's life for all these years, and it would be still to the very end, whatever might be the cost.

In following the Lord Jesus there was "tribulation" to experience, it was true, but there was also a "kingdom" to be possessed, and so there could be "endurance" in time of testing. He bore up under it all because he had so much to gain—so much to *inherit*—in the world to come. Whatever the hostile forces of evil arrayed against him, he could *overcome* them through the strength of his Saviour and Lord.

Now, at length, John is drawing his last book—God's last book—to its exhilarating conclusion. After a long series of startling visions have been recorded—visions disclosing events which are consummated by the establishment of the Saviour's kingdom—John is permitted to glimpse the new, eternal world that God will finally make.

"And I saw a new heaven and a new earth," John writes, "for the first heaven and the first earth were passed away, and there was no more sea. And I, John, saw the holy city, new Jerusalem, coming down from God out of heaven, prepared as a bride arrayed for her husband. And I heard a great voice out of heaven saying, 'Behold, the dwelling-place of God is with men, and He will live with them, and they shall be His people, and God Himself shall be with them. And God shall wipe away all tears from their eyes; and there shall be no more death, nor sorrow, nor crying. Neither shall there be any more pain; for the former things are passed away' " (Rev 21:1-4).

It was a staggering vision! Heaven come down to earth! The God of heaven living among men! And all of the miseries

that once marred the world—death and sorrow, tears and pain
—were banished, and banished forever! It was almost too good
to be true.

But it *was* true. And the next words John heard confirmed
it. "And He that sat upon the throne said, 'Behold, I make all
things new.' And He said unto me, 'Write! For these words
are true and dependable' " (Rev 21:5).

John had almost hesitated to record the vision he had seen,
so splendid it was. But the divine voice said, "Write! You can
depend on it, I *am* making everything new!" And that voice
was the voice of Him who sat on the throne of the universe,
whose workmanship the universe was to begin with. And, if
He made it once, He could make it over again! In fact, that
was the promise His words contained. He would make afresh
what He had made before. And those words were "true and dependable."

"And He said unto me, It is done. I am the Alpha and
Omega, the beginning and the end" (Rev 21:6).

All of the letters of the Greek language, in which the apostle
John was writing, with all of their capacity to express reality,
come between alpha and omega. And all of the events of
history came between history's beginning and its ending. But
God is the Alpha and the Omega, and He is the beginning
and the end. *He* stands, as it were, at the beginning of earth's
temporal experience, and He stands also at its consummation.
It was He who had made the world, and it was He who would
end it that He might make it anew. Thus He sovereignly over-
shadowed the events of all history—from their beginning to
their end—that He might realize His own purposes therein,
and all that might accurately be said in man's language about
the significance of those events must be said in reference to
Him—the Alpha and the Omega!

That too was why John need not hesitate to write the vision
he had seen. The eternal One easily spanned all temporal experience, as He also spanned all temporal knowledge. Whatever

might be known with certainty about the future could be traced directly to the perfect knowledge of the Alpha and Omega. Whatever guarantees there were that this future would come to pass could be traced to the perfect sovereignty of the Beginning and the End. In short, God—and God alone—could both reveal and guarantee man's destiny.

And every individual man has a destiny, and the voice John heard went on to describe it.

"To the one who is thirsty, I will give from the spring of the water of life freely" (Rev 21:6).

That was the first category of man whose future was determined, the *thirsty* man who drank at God's spring. John needed no explanation of the meaning of this, for he still remembered Sychar and Jacob's well. Living water was available at God's fountain, and John knew that the vibrant expression, "water of life," was to be traced directly to the Saviour's words to the Samaritan woman.

She, certainly, had been among the thirsty that day—so thirsty, in fact, that she was utterly prepared to drink this water if she only knew where it could be found. "If you had known the gift of God and who it was that said to you, 'Give me a drink,' you would have asked from Him and He would have given you living water" (Jn 4:10). And she had satisfied her thirst on that occasion—satisfied it perfectly and forever, for in addition the Lord Jesus had also said, "Whoever drinks of the water that I shall give him shall not get thirsty forever. But the water that I shall give him shall become in him a spring of water gushing up into eternal life" (Jn 4:14).

There had been no special conditions attached to that offer, no demands for the reformation of her twisted life, nothing in fact but the simple offer of a wondrous gift. And the offer John had just heard from the Alpha and Omega was the same now at the *end* of God's revelation in Jesus Christ as it had been at the very *beginning*. It was still a gift. "To the one who is thirsty, I will give from the spring of the water of life *freely!*"

But there was a second category of men whose destiny must be described. The voice from the throne went on to do so, as John recorded His words. "The one who overcomes shall inherit these things."

Again, John needed no special instruction. As he had heard his Master offer the gift of life so freely, so he had heard Him offer an inheritance at great cost. Though eternal life was bestowed on any thirsty soul who wished it, the wealth of the future age belonged only to those who lived for God victoriously. To every believer who was born into the family of God there would surely come as inevitably as nighttime follows day, the storms of testing and the allurements of a gaudy, temporal world. And these the believer in Jesus was summoned to confront and to overcome.

For the call of the Saviour was to a life of self-denial and self-sacrifice, in which troubles were endured for Him and the beguilements of this age refused. The one who wished to preserve his earthly life would lose it, while the one who gave it up for Jesus' sake would save it. The pathway of discipleship, therefore, was the pathway of the cross, and in that pathway there must be self-surrender and poverty of spirit.

Unlike the gift of living water, appropriated once for all, such an experience was a continuing commitment entered into day by day. It was nothing less than a constant participation in the Master's own unrivaled food—to do the will of God and to finish His work!

Eternal life is *free*. Discipleship is immeasurably hard. The former is attained by faith alone, the latter by a faith that *works*. The former brings with it the righteousness of God so that a man is "justified freely by His grace" (Ro 3:24). The latter developed a personal righteousness, based on good deeds, so that a man was also "justified by works" (Ja 2:24). The former constituted the believer God's workmanship, the latter fulfilled the wondrous purpose for which he had been created. The former cost man nothing, the latter could cost him everything, including life itself. Thus the former assured man his entrance into God's kingdom, but the latter assured him of *heirship* there.

"The one who *overcomes* shall *inherit* these things." Such was the pronouncement from the throne. There could be no illusions in the matter. God would give living water to a thirsty soul without conditions. But He granted ownership of the world to come only to those who were victorious.

And how splendid was the prospect! New heavens, new earth! A brilliant, celestial city, descending from above, radiant with the exquisite beauty of a bride gorgeously adorned for her husband. Oh, to really *possess* these things! To enjoy them to the limitless fullness of their infinite potential! To be able to say, in that day, not merely, "I am here!" but "These are *mine!*"

The price was high. Jesus had never been vague on *that* point. But it was more—unspeakably more—than worth it! In such an inheritance there was *real* worth, and no fleeting treasure on earth could for a moment be compared with it.

"The one who overcomes shall inherit these things, and I shall be God to him and he shall be a son to Me."

Heirship and sonship! The two concepts were inseparably intertwined, John knew. And the word for "son" which the voice from the throne now called upon the apostle to write, was a word he had never before used in this way. Before, in all of the inspired works that John had written—one gospel, three letters, and now this book of prophecy—this word, when used of relationship to God, had been reserved most strictly for the Lord Jesus Christ Himself. *He* was God's "Son" in a unique and special sense, and believers in Him were never so called in any utterance John had recorded up to now.

Instead, when he wished to designate believers in Jesus as those who had been begotten by God and so possessed eternal life, he had formerly always availed himself of another Greek word for "son," a word which simply meant a "child." Thus in the language of this writer, up to this very moment, Jesus was God's "Son" and Christians were God's "children." But in the world to come, the divine voice had now announced, the "heirs" would be treated as God's "sons."

The thought was richly suggestive. John knew that in the temporal world around him a child could not obtain the inheritance that was his until he reached the age of civil responsibility as established by recognized custom and law. He might be *potentially* rich through all the years of his youth, but when the "child" became a full grown "son" his potential wealth could become *actual* wealth, and he could enter into legal possession of his inheritance. Thus the words of the Alpha and Omega, to which John listened, were fraught with meaning.

According to that special concept of things which it was granted to this particular apostle to write down, "sonship" belonged only to the overcomer. All who drank of the water of life John called "children." But the matured, well-rounded experience to which that relationship could lead belonged only to those who overcame. They were the heirs, because they were the full-grown "sons."

True, John was aware that a beloved fellow apostle named Paul had been in the habit of calling *all* God's children both "heirs" and "sons." And of course John realized that they were, from one point of view. If one thought of salvation itself as an inheritance, freely given to all who believed in Christ, there was every validity to Paul's conception. But John had not been trained by the Master to think of things from that point of view. Paul had become a Christian after the Saviour had left the earth to return for a time to the glory of heaven and after He had poured out the special gift of the Holy Spirit upon all who believed in Him. Paul had never known what it was to follow the Saviour on earth, as John himself had known it. It was natural, therefore, for Paul's perspective to be different.

Indeed, God's truth was too large and too grand to be comprehended from only a single vantage point, and John long ago had recognized the enrichment Paul's doctrine had brought to the Christian church. Still, John was a product of the Saviour's special training and, for him, heirship was confined to "possessing" the kingdom and universe over which Christ would reign.

Paul knew about that kind of heirship, too. And although he spoke of an heirship possessed by all believers into whose heart the Spirit of God had come, he spoke also of a "joint-heirship" with Christ which is predicated on suffering (Ro 8: 16-17). In fact, near the end of his own life—so full of affliction for Christ—he could write, "If we endure in suffering, we shall also reign with Him. If we deny Him, He also will deny us. If we believe not, yet He remains faithful, He cannot deny Himself" (2 Ti 2:12-13). The apostle John might just as easily have written those words as Paul.

Reigning with Christ, Paul declared, depends on our enduring through suffering for Him. After all, the kingdom He shares with us is His because He Himself suffered to gain it. But the privilege of sharing that reign will be denied to us if we fail Him down here. If we turn from Him in shame in this age, He will turn from us in shame in the age to come. "For whoever shall be ashamed of Me and of My words," Jesus had said, "of him shall the Son of man be ashamed, when He shall come in His own glory, and in His Father's, and in that of the holy angels" (Mk 8:38). To be *denied* in that day, to be refused recognition and honor, would be a painful experience indeed.

Yet, there was also a word of comfort. "If we believe not," Paul had added, "yet He remains faithful, He cannot deny Himself." Suppose indeed that instead of bearing up under our trials, our faith collapsed—as in fact it *did* collapse in those whose hearts were like stony ground. What then? Was that the end of our relationship to Him? Far from it! *We* might change, He could not. Whatever promises He had made to us, whatever gifts His grace had bestowed, to these He remained resolutely faithful. To do otherwise would be a denial of His own word, a denial of all that He was; indeed, it would be a denial of Himself. And, He could not deny Himself. No, there was no question of retracting the gift of eternal life He had so unconditionally bestowed. Such a thing was unthinkable. As Paul had elsewhere affirmed, "The gifts and calling of God are irrevocable!" (Ro 11:29).

So Paul and John were in basic harmony, taught as they both were by the same Spirit of God. Yet John, who had been privileged to be so intimate with the earthly Jesus, had always—up until this climactic moment—reserved the concept of sonship to God for the Saviour alone. Now, under the direction of that voice from the throne, he must widen it to include as well the "overcomers," the heirs of the future world. The implications of this were wonderful. To those who lived victoriously on earth, there would be granted—as an integral part of their heirship—a relationship to God similar in character to the relationship sustained to Him by the Lord Jesus Christ Himself.

Even as he penned the words on the papyrus sheet before him, John recalled some earlier words his Master had given him to write which were now rich with meaning. "He who overcomes," the risen Jesus had said to John, "and who keeps My works to the end, to him will I give power over the nations, and he shall rule them with a rod of iron. As the vessels of a potter they shall be broken to pieces, *even as I received from My Father*" (Rev 2:26-27). And again, the exalted Saviour had said, "To him who overcomes will I grant to sit with Me in My throne, *even as I also overcame and am set down with My Father in His throne*" (Rev 3:21).

No, there was no mistaking it. The portion of the overcomer was like the portion of the Son of God Himself in relation to His heavenly Father. As the Father had given His victorious Son a throne and authority over mankind, so in a future day that throne and that authority would be shared with other victorious "sons" as well. *They* were the heirs of God's kingdom or, as Paul would put it, "joint-heirs with Christ."

Accordingly, they had fully realized the potential that was latent in taking that priceless drink of the water of life. By means of that drink they had become God's children forever, but they had not stopped there. Feeding on the food of discipleship, facing and overcoming their earthly ordeals of suffering and deprivation, they had grown to full-fledged sonship to the living God. They had entered an experience with Him that was modeled after the experience of Jesus Christ Himself.

Thus they had touched, in a very special way, the ultimate reality of all that God could be to men. Now, in a superlatively deep and meaningful sense, He was *God* to them. He was, of course, the God of all creation, nor could He cease to be—at any time—the God of every creature. But to the overcomer, He was *God* in a way He could not be to any other thing He had created. For now the overcomer shared the royal privileges of God's own unique, eternal Son. It was, therefore, a wonderful word that had emanated from the throne. It had conveyed an unforgettable promise. "He who overcomes shall inherit these things, and I shall be 'God' to him and he shall be a 'son' to Me!"

Hitherto the divine voice had spoken out the destiny of two classes of men. To those who were thirsty He offered the water of eternal life most freely. That was the gift of God. But to those who did more than drink it, to those who *also* overcame, He offered heirship and sonship in the world to come. And that was *not* a gift! It must be won midst the struggles and hardships of a life devoted to the Lord Jesus and to doing the will of God. But what of those who belonged to neither of these classes? What of those who not only did not overcome, but did not even drink God's living water? How could *their* fate be appropriately described?

The voice continued. "But the fearful, and unbelieving, and the abominable, and murderers, and fornicators, and sorcerers, and idolaters, and all liars, shall have their part in the lake which burns with fire and brimstone, which is the second death" (Rev 21:8).

It was an awful pronouncement. For this was hell, the tragic, eternal abode of all who had no true thirst for the living God. Having spurned or neglected the fountain of the water of life, they will find themselves one day in a fiery lake of death. All chance of quenching any kind of thirst at all would then be gone forever. Even the sinful deeds and desires that eternally stamped the character of those who were there could no longer find any kind of realization in a habitat where suffering alone remained. There was no water in that lake! Only the fires of God's righteous judgment, and an endless existence so worthless and empty that it did not merit even the *name* of "life." And hence, it must be called "the second death."

In the temporal world, John knew, man was always faced with the twin realities of life and death. So it would be also in the eternal world. Life there would be for those who had wisely appropriated it ahead of time, death for those who had not. The former was an endless experience in the presence of a living God. The latter was an endless experience outside of His presence, an existence that had lost all meaning. The former guaranteed man's eternal well-being and, if he overcame, eternal privilege. The latter offered only eternal anguish.

Clearly, then, the fountain of life and the lake of death were the unmistakable alternatives of human destiny. The man who drank of the fountain acquired an inwardly flowing stream which, Jesus had promised, would never cease to gush forth its renewing waters. The man who entered the lake entered an abode of dreadful stagnation. It was the ultimate stanching of every vital spring which makes human existence bearable or worthwhile. It was the final termination of all usefulness, of all joy, and of all hope. It was hell. And it was also a *second* death.

The roster of those who would find their "part" there, however, included none who were not fully worthy of a destiny so dreadful. And strikingly, John noted, that roster began with "the fearful." Fearful? How many there were, John knew from experience, whose hearts and minds cringed with dread from the terrible unknown that, to them, lay just beyond the grave. The thought of death and the gloomy mist that shrouded the world to come were torments which they did their best to evade and to forget. The wonderful message of life, the striking revelation of God's love displayed in the death of His Son for sinful men—these were realities that could not penetrate such faltering hearts.

Their blind, unreasoning fear, therefore, had driven them *away* from God instead of *to* Him. They had submerged themselves in an obviously temporal world, dreading the day of their death but never preparing for it, till at last they found themselves submerged—forever—in a lake of fire. Who could say they were not worthy of their fate? God's Son had come and had offered them life, and instead of rejoicing in His love and accepting His gift, they had simply been afraid.

But next on the solemn roll of hell's inhabitants were the "unbelieving." Obviously, John thought, these were the spiritual brothers of those who were "fearful." Indeed, the fearful had been unbelieving, but there was also an unbelief that was separate from fear. And whether it arose from a stubborn skepticism that was capable of questioning truth however impressively attested, or from a pride of intellect and learning which found God's grace too simple or too foolish to accept— or, in fact, whether it arose from any source whatever—its end was still the same. The unbelieving, as well as the fearful, had their portion forever in the lake of fire.

So also did the "abominable." It was right, John felt instinctively, that they should be mentioned next. For the fear and unbelief which drove man from God, and drove him from God's salvation, were like poisonous roots from which every degrading and disgusting thing in human life could grow. In fact, if a man's character could with any truth be called abominable, it was certain that he in some way lacked confidence and faith in God. A repulsive life was always the misshapen sculpture of a fearful or unbelieving heart.

The rest of the list was in essence a commentary on the forms which the abominable life may take. Hell will be peopled by those who destroy the lives of others, "murderers"; it will be populated by those who distort the physical drive by which human life is reproduced, "fornicators"; it will be inhabited by those who probe beyond life's proper boundaries to seek contact with the unseen powers of evil round about, "sorcerers"; it will be dwelt in by those who misrepresent the author of life or put some human substitute in the place which belongs alone to Him, "idolaters"; and, in particular, it will be the home of all who distort reality, "all liars."

John knew, of course, even as he transcribed this list, that the voice from the throne was describing to him the character of men as it was finally and unalterably fixed by their rejection of the gift of life. It was true enough that all of the evils that the list contained had been found somewhere, sometime among those who would ultimately enter the kingdom of God, even among those who would ultimately inherit that kingdom. But *their* basic character was not determined by their sin. It was determined rather by the grace of God.

"Don't you know," the apostle Paul had once written, "that the unrighteous shall not inherit the kingdom of God? Don't be deceived! Neither fornicators, nor idolaters, nor adulterers, nor homosexuals, nor sodomites, nor thieves, nor covetous, nor drunkards, nor revilers, nor swindlers, shall inherit the kingdom of God. *And such were some of you,* but you have been washed, but you have been sanctified, but you have been justified, in the name of the Lord Jesus and by the Spirit of our God" (1 Co 6:9-11).

The apostle's meaning was clear. Terms like these could no longer be truly and fully applied to his Christian readers. But it was not that they did not *deserve* to have them applied, even then. Paul knew quite well that the believers to whom he wrote were full of unattractive qualities. There was even a case of incest in the church, for which he had indignantly reproved them (1 Co 5:1-2). And immediately before penning his catalogue of the unrighteous who could not inherit God's kingdom, Paul had charged these believers themselves with unrighteous behaviour of their own. "Nay," he wrote, "you act unrighteously and you rob, and you do these things to your brothers!" (1 Co 6:8). Yet in his next breath he could say, "But you have been washed, but you have been sanctified, but you have been justified, in the name of the Lord Jesus and by the Spirit of our God."

How rich and unfailing was the apostle's concept of the gift of God! His readers had been "justified freely" by God's grace, and were the privileged possessors of "the righteousness of God" which was "unto all and upon all them who believe" (Ro 3:21-26). Nothing could change that fact, however miserable their failures might be. And it was Paul's manner to challenge his Christian converts, not by dangling them over a hell from which God's grace had saved them, but by an appeal to live in accordance with what they now were through that grace.

So he very soon warns them of the terrible snare of fornication, and he does *not* threaten them with everlasting damnation, but pointedly asks ,"Don't you know that your bodies are the members of Christ? Shall I, then, take the members of Christ, and make them members of a prostitute? God forbid!" (1 Co 6:15). And a few sentences on, he says, "What? Don't you know that your body is the temple of the Holy Spirit who is in you, whom you have from God, and you are not your own? For you have been bought with a price. Therefore, glorify God in your body and in your spirit which are God's" (1 Co 6:19-20).

No higher or more effective appeal could be found. Psychologically a man behaves according to the self-image he seeks to maintain. And in the mirror of the word of truth, as James would have put it, the believer in Jesus sees the "face he was born with." He sees in God's Word the outline and reflection of that new personality which is now his as one begotten by the Father of lights. He is God's workmanship, a kind of firstfruits of His creatures, and in accordance with that basic reality alone will he find adequate motivation to live a holy life.

Paul knew this and calls upon his fellow Christians constantly to "walk worthy of the calling" with which they had been called by God's grace (Eph 4:1; Col 1:10; 1 Th 2:12). Would they see fornication in its true light? Let them see it as a thing utterly detestable to one whose body has become the temple of a living God!

And would they know how inappropriate unrighteous behavior was for them now that they were justified in the name of the Lord Jesus? Let them be reminded that those who could properly be called fornicators or idolaters or similar things were utterly excluded from an inheritance in God's kingdom. Their "part" (inheritance) was in a lake that burned with fire and brimstone; not so those who were washed and sanctified by the Spirit of our God! Inheritance in God's kingdom was a vital, vibrant hope for them. And so, Paul implies, let them live as those who wish to acquire that inheritance, not as those who have no hope of it.

Yes, John realized, the catalogue of the citizens of hell was a catalogue of those unwashed, unsanctified, unjustified by the bountiful gift of God. God saw a man in either one of two ways. Either He saw him as His own workmanship, a kind of firstfruits of His creatures, a possessor of righteousness freely given by His grace; or He saw him as fearful or unbelieving or abominable or whatever else a sinful life had made him. Those who accepted God's gift and thus were His workmanship could inherit the future kingdom. But those who had never accepted that gift could inherit nothing but a lake of fire. "But the fearful, and unbelieving, and the abominable, and murderers, and fornicators, and sorcerers, and idolaters, and all liars, *shall have their part* in the lake which burns with fire and brimstone, which is the second death!"

If such was the grim reality confronted by those who died in their sins, never having tasted the water of life, it was inevitable that the final book of God's holy Word should sound one last call to men to partake of that water. And it was fitting that John, who had recorded the initial appeal at Sychar's well, should be chosen to pen this one as well. To him, it seemed, belonged the writing of the alpha and the omega, the beginning and the end of the Saviour's offer of living water.

John had just reached his last sheet of papyrus, and now the voice he heard speaking to him was explicitly that of the same person who had leaned wearily on Jacob's well so many years ago. Its tones and inflections were the same—John knew them well—but they now possessed a resonance which they had lacked that day from a tired and thirsty Saviour. He had been a real man down here on earth, just as He was a real man up there in heaven, though partaking now of the vitality of a resurrected life.

The Risen One was speaking. "I, Jesus, have sent My angel to testify these things to you in the churches. I am the root and the offspring of David, the bright, the morning star."

The unfolding of precious revelations for the instruction of Christian churches was now at an end. And the voice which attested them was the voice of one who was both God and man. He was the root of David, because He was David's Maker, but He was also David's descendant. In fact, years ago on the occasion of the announcement of His coming birth, the angel of God had said to Mary, "He shall be great, and shall be called the Son of the Highest, and the Lord God shall give to Him the throne of His father David and He shall reign over the house of Jacob forever, and of His kingdom there shall be no end" (Lk 1:32-33). So this was His destiny as the offspring of David, and it was this that made Him mankind's greatest hope. In a world swathed in the darkness of sin and in ignorance of its Maker, He was the Morning Star, the herald of a new day and a new world, when earth's darkest hours would be relieved at last by His coming and His kingdom. But in the meanwhile, there was a message to get out.

The voice of Jesus continued. "And the Spirit and the bride say, 'Come.' And let him who hears say, 'Come.' And the one who is thirsty, let him come. And whoever wishes, let him take the water of life freely" (Rev 22:17).

John felt a slight lump in his throat as he wrote those words. The years had not dimmed at all his profound appreciation of God's gift, and in his mind's eye he could still see his Master talking with the woman of Samaria as he and his fellow disciples returned with their purchases from Sychar. How shocked they had been at that sight! But it wasn't long before they had realized, through the Saviour's skillful instruction about spiritual food, that He had been saying "Come!" to that woman and that He wanted His disciples to say it too. He wanted them to say "Come!" to everyone He sent them to, and to broadcast far and wide the availability of His living water. That was the message of God's Holy Spirit. That would be the message of the whole Christian church, Christ's bride (Eph 5:25-32).

And that *should* be the message of anyone at all who heard it. It was a glorious communication! Only the dull of heart could fail to pass it on. And no one could be *that* dull of heart and be a true disciple at the same time.

To say "Come!" to a needy world of men was the disciples' surpassing responsibility. And to say it consistently and faithfully through life often involved toil and sacrifice and suffering. But it was also an unspeakable privilege, a thrilling and invigorating experience, like the eating of some celestial food. And it *was* celestial food! The Lord of glory Himself had eaten it while here on earth, and those who hungered to know more of Him and to possess the eternal world over which He would someday reign, could eat it too. *He* had said "Come!" to them, *they* could say "Come" to others.

But though discipleship, as taught by the Lord Jesus, was invariably associated with this kind of obedience to God's will and with finishing this kind of work for Him, the water of life was invariably associated with God's unconditional generosity. The poor woman who stood before the Saviour and the well that day—so unworthy she might seem even to hear His offer— was precisely the type of person who best exemplified what the grace of God really is. Had her life been in the least degree a worthy one, the lesson might not have been so clear. Moreover, had she been asked to make it worthy, the lesson would not have been clear either. For the lesson involved a gift. And with a gift, there can be no bargaining, only giving and receiving.

And just now, as a resurrected Jesus spoke for the last time of living water, there was no trace of a bargain. "And he who is thirsty, let him come. And whoever wishes, let him take of the water of life freely." No special, meritorious qualifications were laid down, no binding commitments for the future. Who could take this water? The one who was thirsty! But was even *that* too strong? Well then, simply the one who *wants* to! "Whoever wishes—let him take!"

Salvation could not be made simpler. Nor clearer. Eternal life for the taking. And the only ones left out are those who do not want it. It was, therefore, the perfect bestowal fulfilling man's highest conception of what a gift should be—totally, unspeakably, utterly *free!*

"If thou knewest the gift of God, and who it is that saith to thee, Give me to drink; thou wouldest have asked of him, and he would have given thee living water." And she *had* asked of Him and He *had* given her that thirst-quenching water.

But then the hunger began! The hunger to go back into that little village and to say to its men, "Come!" *"Come, see a man, which told me all things that ever I did: is not this the Christ?"*

But it was all perfectly natural. Her thirst had led her to eternal life, and her hunger would lead her to eternal heirship. That is the appropriate experience for everyone who believes in the Lord Jesus. For after all, the thirsty live, but the hungry inherit!